THE FANTASTIC FIFTIES

The 1950s were the heyday of the 'pulps'. Cheap paperback production after the war enabled a slew of 'poverty row' publishing houses in the US to capitalise on the public's prurient appetite for sensation, be it science fiction aliens or sleazy detective mysteries, through books and magazines printed on 'pulp' paper and wrapped in lurid covers featuring half-naked girls at the mercy of both monsters and mobsters. From *Amazing Stories* and *True Adventures* to *Thrilling Wonder Stories*, *Popular Detective* and *Man's Life*, the pulps mushroomed in bookstores like a literary virus. The British publishing industry was less willing to stoop so low and merely adopted the same cheap and efficient manufacturing methods to bring the classics to the masses in more accessible paperback form. The paperback revolution led to a revival of the short story, which had long been a staple of fiction writers, and anthologies in the horror, ghost, sci-fi and mystery genres became commonplace. The wonder is that more of these short stories did not reach the big screen - television, with its penchant for half-hour series episodes, scooped up plenty of them for the likes of *Alfred Hitchcock Presents* or *The Twilight Zone*. Of those that did make it, George Langelaan's 'The Fly' is probably the most notable. Both 'The Fly' and Carl Stephenson's 'Leiningen Versus the Ants', which had already been adapted to the screen as *The Naked Jungle* in 1954, were reprinted in Pan's popular Books of Horror Stories in the early Sixties, but the only other examples of short horror fiction to follow them into cinemas were the numerous tales of Edgar Allen Poe and the collected works of Robert Bloch, when Amicus Films latched onto the writer of *Psycho* later in the same decade.

The tragedy of this is that there was a rich vein of original material available in print for filmmakers to adapt, but the usual commercial myopia prevented anyone from spotting the possibilities; the industry, on both side of the Atlantic, preferred as ever to play it safe than try to attempt something new. And yet three of the most enduring hits of the 1950s - *The Beast From 20,000 Fathoms*, *It Came From Outer Space* and the Delmer Daves' western *3:10 to Yuma* - had all derived from short stories, that last from the pen of Elmore Leonard. Screenwriters no doubt found it easier to condense a novel to the needs of a movie than to enlarge upon a short story, though perhaps the most striking example of what could be done with the medium also came about in the 1960s, when Arthur C Clarke's 'The Sentinal' served as the basis for Stanley Kubrick's *2001: A Space Odyssey*. Having been sidelined in the 1970s with the resurgence of the popular novel, the short story has yet to experience a renaissance in any meaningful way; in the meantime, our lead article in this issue is a reminder of the original thinking that could be found within the form. All this and monsters too in the magazine with a difference... ***The Fantastic FIFTIES***.

THE FANTASTIC FIFTIES / Issue #9 **Winter 2019**
Editor: Denis Meikle / *editor@hemlockpublishing.com*
Advertising/Enquiries: Jane Meikle / *info@hemlockpublishing.com*
The Fantastic Fifties contributors: Sarah Appleton, Allan Bryce, Simon Fitzjohn, Bruce Hallenbeck, John Hamilton, Richard Holliss, Richard Klemensen, Christopher Koetting, Andrew Llewellyn, Rod Labbe, Mark McGee, Kevin Nickelson, Jim O'Brien, Simon Pritchard, Jonathan Rigby, Brian Robb, Bryan Senn, Ian Taylor, Ian White, Mark Wolf
Special photographic contributions: *BigScreenGoodies.com* (Bob Villard)
The Fantastic Fifties is published three times a year (spring, summer, autumn/winter) by Hemlock Publishing, a division of **Hemlock Books Limited:**
Hemlock Hall, Goodwin Close, Hailsham BN27 3DE *(01323) 442669*
The Fantastic Fifties online: *www.hemlockbooks.co.uk/Shop/category/16*
Printed and bound by Sussex Print Services, Seaford, East Sussex BN25 3LH

CONTENTS / No 9

Denis Meikle teams up with Vincent Price to find what the buzz was about when Patricia Owens used a steam-press on her husband's head...

'Did you say that André is at the factory?'
'Yes...under the steam-hammer.'
'Under the what?'
'The steam-hammer! But don't ask so many questions. Please come quickly François. Please understand that I'm afraid...that my nerves won't stand it much longer.'

--George Langelaan, The Fly (1957)

IN 1958, the boom in apocalyptic science-fiction films which Paramount had effectively set in motion with *When Worlds Collide* (1951) and *The War of the Worlds* (1953) was still going strong, although it had now been accentuated by monster-fare of an increasingly disparate kind since Warner Brothers unleashed *Them!* in 1954. In the face of the overwhelming popularity of a plethora of such films from a revitalised Universal-International, such as *This Island Earth* (1956), *The Incredible Shrinking Man* (also 1956) and *Invasion of the Body Snatchers* (1957), others opted to join the bandwagon. Of the remaining studios which comprised the Hollywood 'Big 5', M-G-M had taken the plunge with

Forbidden Planet (1956) - only Twentieth Century Fox, under then-President Spyros P Skouras, had so far managed to resist the trend, preferring to stick with its familiar diet of period costumers, musicals and lush romantic melodramas.

Fox's big hit of 1958 was to be the roadshow spectacular *South Pacific*, but the continuing threat from television, the expensive technical failure of Cinemascope 55 and a spate of slack financial returns from more conventional product had forced a rethink, and Fox purchased the rights to a short story by George Langelaan which had been published in *Playboy* magazine in June 1957. The studio was not averse to farming an occasional exploitation programmer out to one of several 'shadow' companies, such as that run by B-movie producer and one-time theatre owner Robert L Lippert, where involvement was limited to distribution only. On this occasion, however, the wily Fox decided to put its corporate logo where its money was going.

'The Fly' was typical of the kind of horror stories which had come to dominate anthologies of weird tales since the 1930s. An emphasis on physical gruesomeness was the keynote of this new breed of fiction, and the proliferation of paperback publishing after the second world war had seen the more traditional ghost story entirely supplanted by a more visceral stable-mate in the 1950s, though the popularity of the latter was not so universal as that of the former.

Given its format, 'The Fly' unfolds as a tale of mystery rather in the manner of Robert Louis Stevenson's *Strange Case of Dr Jekyll and Mr Hyde*, opening *after* the cessation of the events with which it is really concerned and travelling back in time to unravel the puzzle and supply a satisfactory solution to it.

The story is set in France, and it

Patricia Owens, Charles Herbert, David Hedison

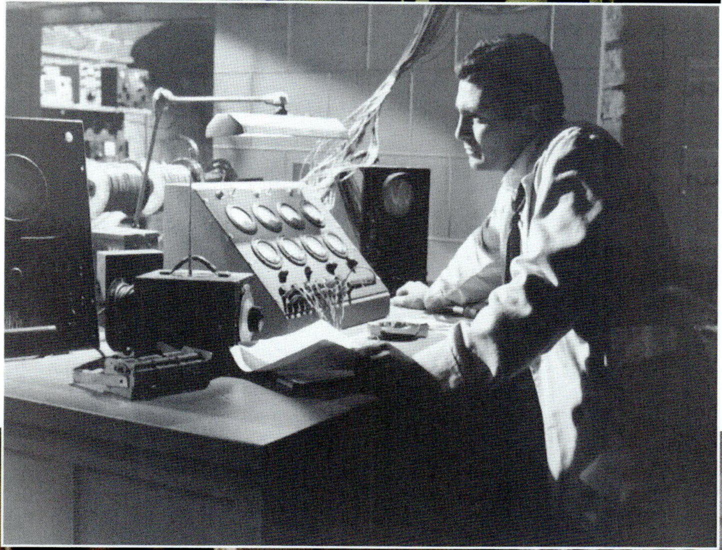

Eugene Borden, Herbert Marshall, Vincent Price, Patricia Owens

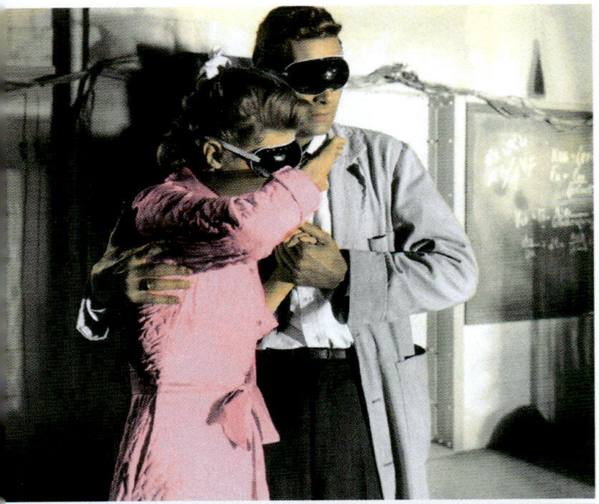

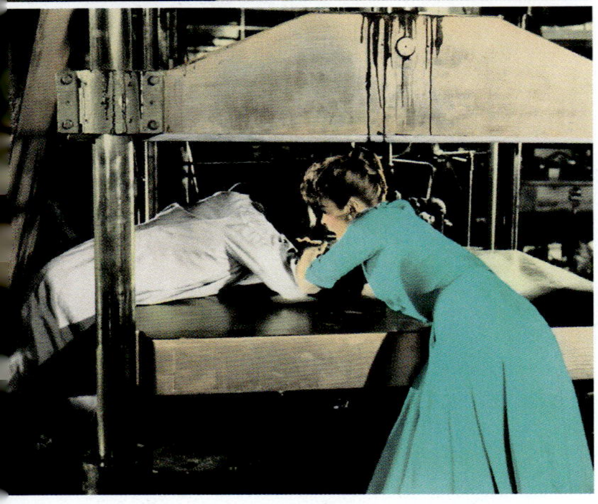

opens with Hélène Delambre informing her brother-in-law Francois that she has just slain her husband by crushing his head in an industrial steam-press, a crime for which she is immediately incarcerated in an insane asylum. As a police investigation gets underway, it transpires that André Delambre, who worked for the French Air Ministry, had been conducting experiments into matter-transference, and that one such experiment had gone mysteriously, but catastrophically, wrong. All is finally revealed in a written statement penned by Hélène prior to her own climactic suicide and read by Francois, who is also the narrator of the tale. In echo of Jekyll's post-mortem confession in the Stevenson story, Hélène reveals that André had experimented on himself in his attempt to disintegrate-reintegrate atoms to another place in space and that during the experiment, a fly had inadvertently been allowed to enter the transmitter and their atoms had intertwined (along with those of an earlier failed attempt on the family cat). André, as a result of this oversight, had ended up with the fly's head (as well as the cat's ear and nose) and, at his own request, Hélène had crushed the offending article under the steam-hammer. Hélène's confession is taken with a large pinch of salt by Commissaire Charras of the Surêté until Francois stumbles upon a fly with a 'white head' which hitherto has flitted in and out of the narrative. Finding it trapped in a spider's web, he crushes it to death - as Hélène had done to its human counterpart - and buries it in a matchbox alongside his brother.

James Clavell's screenplay for the film stuck strictly to the letter of Langelaan's short story, deviating from it only in the matter of Hélène's suicide by cyanide poisoning and the appending of a son to the union of she and André, on the premise that a child might look less foolish than an adult when it came to hunting down an insect with a human head. Despite its

American leads and the domestic nature of the production, the action was relocated to Canada rather than the States, in an effort to accommodate the French names of Langelaan's protagonists.

Vincent Price was cast in the sympathetic but essentially neutral role of Francois Delambre, his name being employed for marquee value in the main, while the role of the title-monster was allocated to Al Hedison, a Fox contract player who was required to spend much of his time onscreen with his features hidden beneath a black silk towel. Another contract star, Michael Rennie (who had helped the company to success with *The Day the Earth Stood Still* in 1951) turned the film down and, despite objections from Fox Head of Production Buddy Adler, Price was brought in to replace him on the strength of the huge grosses that had greeted *House of Wax* five years earlier.

As a high-value studio production of what was essentially a pulp concept, *The Fly* has much to commend it. In line with the times, Langelaan's 'The Fly' was a horror story in science fiction guise, but the film re-emphasised the sci-fi element and confined the horror to its two set-piece scenes: the discovery of André's body under the steam-press - an horrendous image which would remain unrivalled in its stunning impact until the chest-burster of *Alien* more than twenty years later - and Hélène inadvertently stumbling upon the exact nature of the fate which has befallen her unfortunate husband.

The viewer has been well-primed throughout to the probability that André has absorbed the atoms of the fly that has entered his matter-transmitter at the inopportune moment; he *sucks* at his food under cover of a cloth, while his wife is out of sight but still within earshot, and starts to chalk increasingly desperate messages on the blackboard in his lab - 'Brain says strange things now... feel my will going' - before the black pincer that was once his left hand can grab hold of his right to stop him, in scenes which would influence Terry Southern and Stanley Kubrick when they came to create *Dr Strangelove*.

The revelation, when it comes, is nonetheless one of screen's greatest moments of shock: 'I know it's worked!' Hélène exclaims, after André has again tried in vain to reverse the process, and more in hope than belief, as she whips the towel away to reveal a giant fly-head, complete with shimmering eyes, a distended proboscis and twitching antennae, in an unmasking scene to rank alongside those of *The Phantom of the Opera* and *The Mystery of the Wax Museum*.

George Langelaan had conceived it thus: 'The horror was too much for me, too unexpected. As a matter of fact, I am sure that, even had I known, the horror-impact could hardly have been less powerful. Trying to push both hands into my mouth to stifle my screams and although my fingers were bleeding, I screamed again and again. I could not take my eyes off him, I could not even close them, and yet I knew that if I looked at the horror much longer, I would go on screaming for the rest of my life.'

Hélène's screams are magnified by a shot of her face which is intended to emulate the view through the fly's compound-lensed eyes. It is this kaleidoscopic image, as much as the fly-head itself, which fully imparts the hammer-blow: '..her eyes seemed to be screaming with fear', was Langelaan's vision, and nowhere in the history of horror is the written word better translated to the screen: Ben Nye's superb makeup for Al Hedison brings the monster to life in a way that bears striking relation to imagined reality (unlike that in the eventual sequel), and the moment of fright which the sequence engenders as André

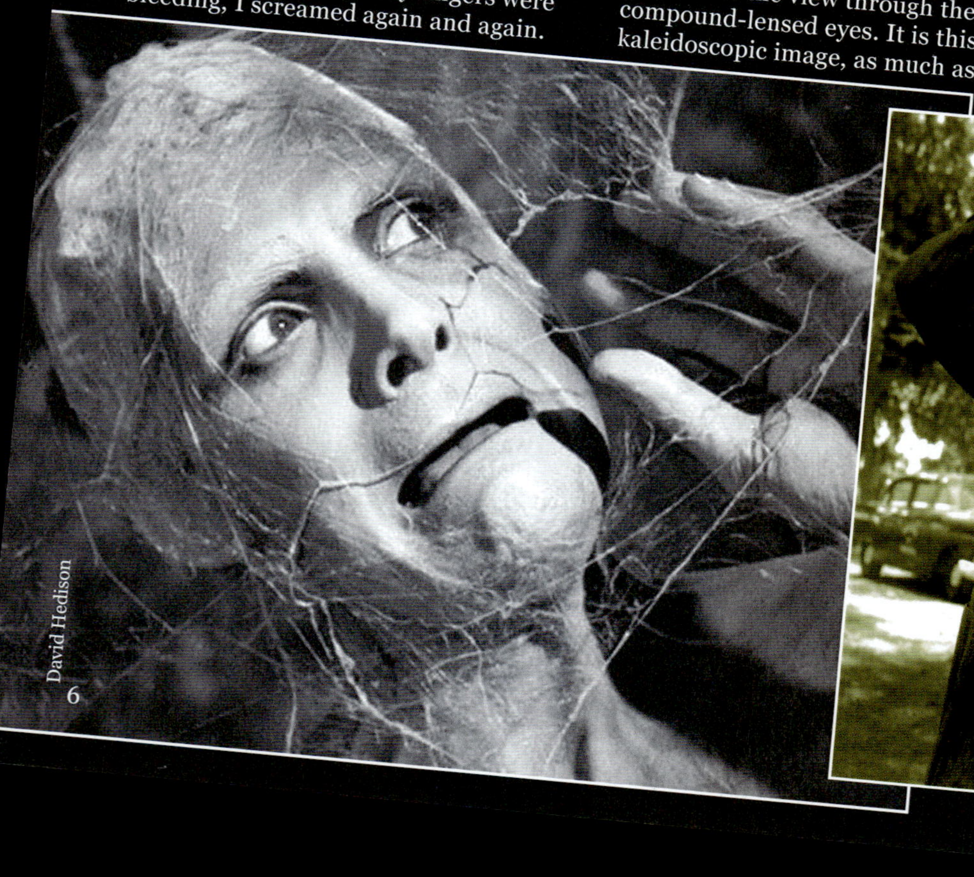

advances, his head jerking involuntarily from side to side, ranks as one of the most overwhelming ever committed to film.

The long and harrowing opening sequence of Hélène crushing André's head and arm in the press is starkly horrific in its clinical staging. At the other end of the scale, the climactic scene in which André the fly screams 'help me!' from the confines of the web may be unintentionally risible, but it makes perfect sense in terms of the internal logic of Clavell's script - as the fly's brain has inexorably subsumed that of the man (a consequence which would be made more of in David Cronenberg's 1986 remake with Jeff Goldblum in the title-role), so André's has taken control of the insect's.

Director Kurt Neumann, who died before the film went into release, makes good use of the scope screen, though oft-repeated scenes of André's laboratory in full matter-transmitting flood ape those in *Forbidden Planet* of only two years before, even to the inclusion of the 'electronic tonalities' which accompany the action. Despite its employment of De Luxe colour and Cinemascopic surface sheen, *The Fly* was something of a throwback to mad-scientist movies of the 1930s and '40s; it was not the start of a new era in science-fiction but the end of an old one. 'There are things man should never experiment with,' André remarks, harking back to the moral philosophies of the pre-atomic age.

Nevertheless, *The People* thought the film was 'so skilfully built up, so well acted, and so taut with terror that the effect is harrowing,' while *Spectator* magazine conceded, somewhat reluctantly, that 'plush horror has arrived; in other words, monstrosity has achieved a kind of respectability which is hardly a pretty thought..'

The film's most unsettling scene comes when André excitedly atomises the family cat, only to find that he cannot reintegrate it again. 'A stream of cat atoms' emit a ghostly meow around the lab and hint metaphorically of the dangers ahead, both for André and for mankind itself. In such interludes did the science fiction films of the fifties truly capture the essence of the 'brave new worlds' to which their protagonists were travelling with both eyes wide shut.

I turned around as the booth door opened.

His head and shoulders still covered with the brown velvet cloth, André was gingerly stepping out of it.

'How do you feel, André? Any difference?' I asked, touching his arm.

He tried to step away from me and caught his foot in one of the stools which I had not troubled to pick up. He made a violent effort to regain his balance, and the velvet cloth slowly slid off his shoulders and head as he fell heavily backwards.

The horror was too much for me, too unexpected. As a matter of fact, I am sure that, even if I had known, the horror-impact could hardly have been less powerful. Trying to push both hands into my mouth to stifle my screams and although my fingers were bleeding, I screamed again and again. I could not take my eyes off him, I could not even close them, and yet I knew that if I looked at the horror much longer, I would go on screaming for the rest of my life...

--George Langelaan, The Fly (1957)

After the first two reels, Price's contribution to the film is minimal and his name attaches to it only in retrospect. The real star of the show is Al Hedison, a Fox contract-player in whom the studio had high hopes and who went from here to *The Lost World* (1960), before adopting his middle-name in place of his first and settling down as David Hedison to a long run in television with *Voyage to the Bottom of the Sea*.

However, the cumulative effect of having featured in two high profile shockers now began to gravitate Price more assuredly towards a career in the macabre. With *The Fly*, sci-fi horror gained respectability; the conventional horror thriller was still to do so. Herbert Marshall's Inspector Charras struggled manfully with the prosthetic left leg which the actor had worn in secret since losing his own in World War II, but less manfully with a screenplay which required him to seek out a fly with a tiny human head. He and Price almost died laughing when it came time to shoot the climax of the film, in which the fly-torsoed André is discovered in a spider's web, headed for ingestion by the local arachnid. They eventually managed to pull it off - just - but not without some cost to the credibility of what had gone before.

The Fly opened in the US in July 1958 and grossed $3 million for Fox from an investment of £350,000. The inevitable sequel followed it into production nine months later, but on that occasion, it was the audiences who were to find themselves dying of laughter when it surfaced in due course.

Despite his subordinate status in *The Fly*, Vincent Price now had two consecutive hits on his hands with his forays into horror, and he was a new and more commanding presence when he took to the stage for the expository opening of *Return of the Fly*.

Reminiscing in later years, Price was characteristically tolerant of one of the

Brett Halsey, Danielle De Metz

low-points of his entire acting career. 'It was actually a better script than *The Fly*,' he remarked of its sequel. 'But the first one had taken the edge off it.' Setting aside the vested interests of an actor when it comes to his own scenes in any specific film, *Return of the Fly* was in no way better than its predecessor. For one thing, it lacked the originality which was the first film's great strength. For another, Price had read only a rough draft of the script before signing to do the film and it was subsequently amended, reducing his role and the costs which would have accrued had it been shot as written.

Fox's lack of interest in pursuing a sequel to *The Fly* was exemplified by the fact that the studio farmed out the production to a subsidiary called Associated Producers in the form of 53-year-old Chicago-born quickie-merchant Edward L Bernds, merely retaining distribution rights in the final product. As a writer, Bernds had been responsible for *World Without End* (1954) and *Queen of Outer Space* (1956) and his previous directorial assignment was *High School Hellcats* (1958), so the one-time sound engineer with Frank Capra (who had worked with The Bowery Boys on *The Bowery Boys Meet the Monsters* in 1954, and who would go on from here to direct The Three Stooges) was not a man whose name might have featured prominently on a short-list to stage a follow-up to the most successful science fiction film of its year had there been any real concern about the outcome. But Like André Delambre's in *The Fly*, Fox's collective mind was currently elsewhere.

In light of the above, the plot of *Return of the Fly* was strictly grade Z material. André's son Philippe, now grown to manhood, takes up matter-transmission where his father had left off, in the style of the Universal sequels of old. His unsavoury assistant is intent on stealing the secret for himself but when his scheming is exposed, a fight ensues. He knocks Philippe unconscious and attempts to dispose of him by placing him in the disintegrator along with a housefly: Hey Presto! - A man with a fly's head. The 'Fly' pursues the criminals to their lair and kills them both; back in the lab, nice Uncle Francois reverses the transmission process and returns Philippe to his normal self. No marks for originality there, then.

Bernds hired Brett Halsey - of *High School Hellcats* fame - to play the role of Philippe, but apart from Price and John Sutton (who previously had starred alongside Price in *Tower of London* and who was brought in to replace an ailing Herbert Marshall), the remainder of the cast were strictly from hunger. Even the limited participation of the two leads did not allow the film to be shot in colour, though Fox loaned its scope lens to the production.

Price is accorded a strong opening scene, in which he recounts the events of the original to Philippe in what remains of the standing-set from *The Fly* (and after a night-watchman has warned them against entering the lab, as Universal's peasants were inclined to do whenever unwary travellers came within striking distance of Castle Dracula). The Price that filmgoers were coming to expect of his performances in the genre could now be seen to be fully-formed as a result of his recent appearance in *House on Haunted Hill*. Alternately rolling both his eyes and his 'r's, he makes the most of the only good lines in the entire script.

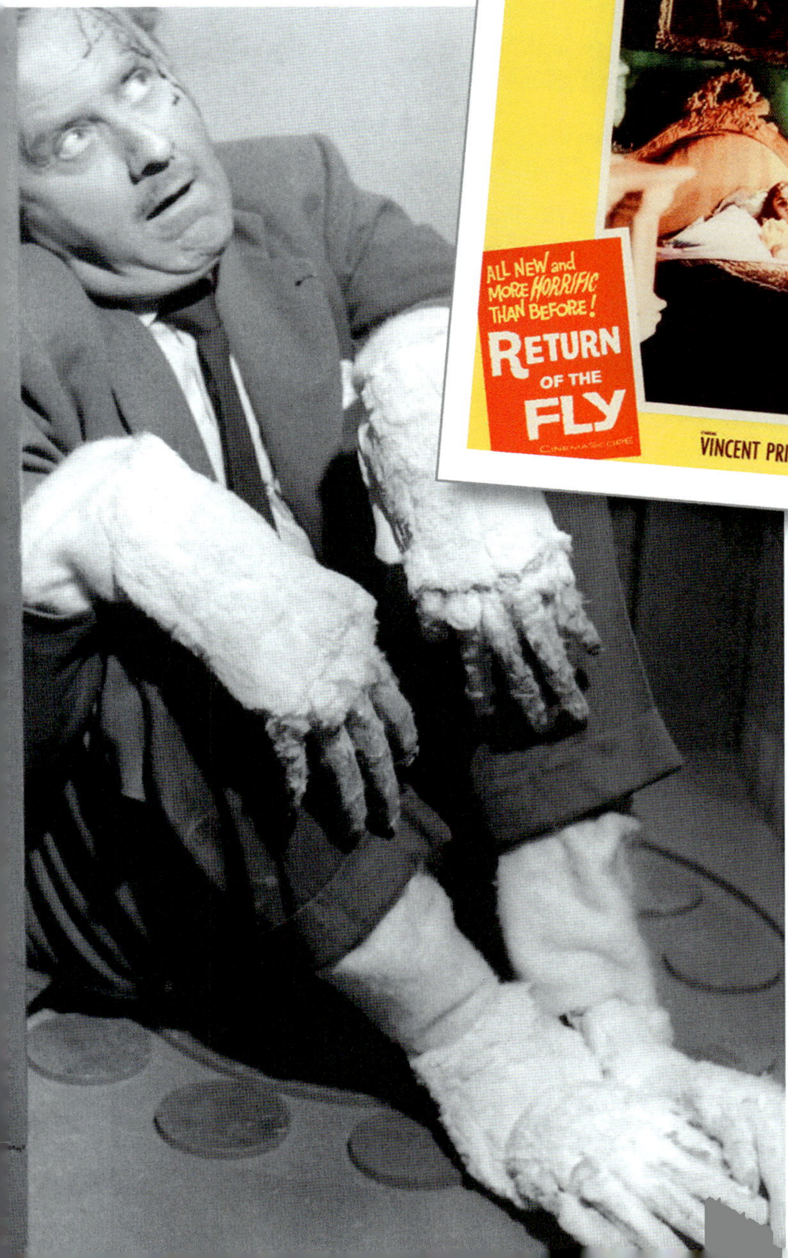

Budget and ingenuity were all used up by this point, however. Philippe soon falls in with a pair of stock villains called Alan and Max - the latter of whom is a mortician and unlikely part-time 'fence.' Nevertheless, he enables the machine to work again with the minor irritant that the reintegration process causes 'giantism' in any non-human participants. When Philippe is inevitably encumbered with the head of a fly, it is ten times the size of that in the original film (presumably to compensate for the lack of colour). With it comes a remarkable insight into the plot which has been hatched against him, and he dishes out a cursory revenge against the dastardly duo before returning to the lab to have the tear in his genes repaired.

Return of the Fly was the polar opposite of the film which had sired it: cheap, careless and crass. From its

Return of the Fly star David Frankham talks about working on the film to Kevin Nickelson...

David Frankham

"I only really knew Brett Halsey for the thirteen days we worked on *Return of the Fly*, but he was very easy to work with and I found him pleasant and low-key. I remember being a bit envious of him for actually being a studio contract player, and thinking that he was a very good actor, which was definitely not the case with some of the "handsome young leading man" types the studios were promoting at the time. In fact, that impression was reinforced just recently when I watched the movie on TCM. I could see Brett really listening and thinking - "acting is listening," you know - and not just waiting for his next line. I thought we worked well together.

He was embarrassed at having to hold his head still while he said, "Help me!" so it could later be put on to a fly. Also, in the movie I had to drive a fancy little convertible. The problem was, as Elizabeth Taylor knew, I couldn't drive at that point. My only driving experience had been being "taught" to drive a jeep for one day in the British Army. The next problem was, that convertible belonged to Brett Halsey, and Brett was understandably very protective of it. He kept hovering about saying, "You do know how to drive stick-shift, don't you, David?" "Sure, sure." Ed Bernds, the director, and a wonderful man, asked if I wanted to run through the action before doing a take, but I said no because I knew that if we did I would have to return the car to its first position, and I didn't know how.

So, there I was sitting in Brett's expensive car waiting for Ed to call "Action", desperately hoping not to wipe out the entire crew.. and who should walk over from another set and start asking me about the car but my Number One singing idol, Bing Crosby, whom I was devoted to from those teenaged years playing records in the kitchen! "I'm sorry, Mr Crosby! I don't know. I'm waiting for them to call action!" So, my hero said, "Oh!" and backed away and I never saw him again. Ed called "Action" and I drove to my spot and stopped without killing the crew and destroying Brett's convertible. The funny end to this story is that not too long ago I told this story on my Facebook page. Among the comments underneath appeared: BRETT HALSEY: "Thanks for not wrecking my car!"

I always think of (director) Ed Bernds as a big gentle giant of a man. I remember he was a quiet man who smiled a lot - but not with a big broad grin William Witney had. It was more an understated smile. It is interesting that two of my favorite directors should have been complete contrasts in terms of personality and directing style, but both were old pros and very well prepared. That's what they had in common. When I auditioned for *Return of the Fly*, for the only time in my career, I walked out of an audition knowing for certain I had the part. Immediately after I read for Ed and Bernard Glasser, they just looked at each, nodded, said, "Okay," and Ed said to me, "David, the part is yours if you want it." I walked out of their office on Cloud Nine.. but then looked at the other poor actors in the waiting

Universal-inspired opening of a doomy visit to a cobweb-encrusted 'mad lab' in the middle of a thunderstorm to its monster-rally finale, it is pure drive-in drivel.

According to writer-director Bernds, Price was disquieted by the quality (or lack of) of his script: 'Some cuts were made to trim it down,' he explained to Price's biographer Lucy Chase Williams. 'Vincent liked some of the scenes we had cut, and he objected.' Producer Bernard Glasser concurred - 'He was not overly enthusiastic about the screenplay'. Price's protestations were hardly surprising: he had been asked to reprise his character of Francois Delambre from *The Fly*, but Francois disappears from the action after the opening reel and only returns at the end to be shot, whereupon he spends the remainder of the story confined to a hospital bed.

In paring down the dialogue and the participation of the leads, half the film's meagre running-time had consequently to be taken up by the activities of more cost-effective extras: in an interminable sequence, Max (Dan Seymour) paces nervously in his funeral-parlour as though literally awaiting direction, two stunt-men (who also alternated in playing the 'Fly'), *twice* the age of the actors whom they are meant to represent, enact the key fight-scene, and sundry policemen mark time for John Sutton's absent Inspector Beecham, in order to spread his few appearances more evenly throughout the production. If budding directors required a lesson on how to hire actors for a few days' work and give the impression that they are in an entire film, *Return of the Fly* is the graduate paper.

Brett Halsey, Vincent Price

No slice of fifties' shlock-horror was complete without its acid repartee, and even Bernds manages to come up with some: when Francois queries Philippe's whereabouts, the man who has just stuffed his body into the matter-transmitter replies, 'That's an interesting question, Mr Delambre - Shall we say he's serving the cause of science.'

As the Fly buzzes unconvincingly around the countryside, the stunt-man occupying the monster-suit in place of Halsey can clearly be seen grappling with the unwieldy mask to stop it from toppling off his shoulders. The only scene that improves on the original is the brief, if risible, superimposition of Halsey's head on a fly's body. As an example of a no-budget 'B' movie, *Return of the Fly* makes *Plan 9 From Outer Space* look like classic sci-fi. 'What if Philippe does not have the mind of a human, but the murderous brain of a fly?' Francois enquires of Beecham in all seriousness. By that time, it has become self-evident that most of those involved in the film had the brain of a fly - but all of them were on the other side of the camera.

room, waiting to audition, knowing I already had the part. Usually I was probably in their position.

On the set Ed gave very little direction to the actors, but having written the script himself, I knew he would give me whatever direction was necessary if I strayed from his idea of the character. I'm flattered he never did. In fact, for the one time in my career, I heard a film crew give applause to the actors. I had just finished the master shot of my funeral home scene with Dan Seymour, whom I was in awe of from all his classic movies. It one of the best-written scenes I ever got to do, and afterward the crew burst into applause. It was Ed who led the applause. I stayed in some touch with Ed Bernds over the years and still have a few letters from him. In one he told me that both he and I had had good careers, but never quite had the breaks to go further and do the kind of work we were really capable of. I found that very touching, and on his part showed a certain balance of self-confidence, but also a kind of humility.'

THE NAKED JUNGLE

PULP HORRORS

The Brazilian official threw up lean and lanky arms and clawed the air with wildly distended fingers. 'Leiningen,' he shouted, 'you're insane! They're not creatures you can fight - they're an elemental - an "Act of God"! Ten miles long, two miles wide - ants, nothing but ants! And every single one of them a fiend from hell; before you can spit three times they'll eat a full-grown buffalo to the bones. I tell you if you don't clear out at once there'll be nothing left of you but a skeleton picked as clean as your own plantation...'

--Carl Stephenson, 'Leiningen Versus the Ants' (1937)

Jim O'Brien treks into the Brazilian jungle to meet Charlton Heston and comes face to fang with 'marabunta' - the deadliest six-legged peril since *Them*...

Charlton Heston, Eleanor Parker

IN 1937, Viennese author and editor Carl Stephenson had a short story, 'Leiningens Kampf mit den Ameisen' (basically, 'Leiningen's War with the Ants'), published in German magazine *Das Neue Linie* (*The New Line*).

The Leiningen of the story is the laconic but courageous owner of a cocoa plantation in the Brazilian rainforest who vows to protect his hard-won Rio Negre estate from the ravages of a vast column of approaching soldier ants. Warned by the District Commissioner that the flesh-eating ants will destroy all in their path, Leiningen declines the Commissioner's offer of escape aboard his riverboat and stubbornly sets about the defence of his house and crops against the seemingly unstoppable insects. Dragooning his wavering plantation workers into an effective fighting force, Leiningen attempts to hold back the besieging creatures with a series of defensive measures. But as the voracious ants continue to gain ground, the plantation owner is finally forced into making a suicidal dash - his clothes soaked in petrol - through the mass of ants, so that he can dynamite a dam and unleash a punitive deluge that will wipe away the invaders once and for all.

Apparently translated by Stephenson himself, the story was then reprinted to popular acclaim in US men's magazine *Esquire* in 1938, its title changed slightly to 'Leiningen versus the Ants'. Following the war, the story was adapted for radio, being broadcast as part of men's high adventure series *Escape* twice in 1948 and then once again in 1949. In both the first two productions, Leiningen was portrayed by actor William Conrad.

Given the story's success in print and on radio it was perhaps inevitable that the Hollywood studios would show interest in Stephenson's yarn and in summer 1953, producer George Pal and director Byron Haskin began work on a movie version for Paramount Pictures. Both Pal and Haskin had backgrounds in animation and special effects and had worked together on *The War of the Worlds* (also at Paramount) in 1952. No doubt the two men felt that their collective experience with effects - Pal's *Destination Moon* (1950) and *When Worlds Collide* (1951) had both won special effects Oscars - would allow them to successfully negotiate the evident challenges presented by the film in convincingly depicting vast swarms of ants rampaging across Brazil.

Pal and Haskin tasked writers Ranald MacDougall and Ben Maddow with developing the

film's script. MacDougall had form as the screenwriter for several significant late '40s *films noir*, including *Mildred Pierce* (1945) and *The Unsuspected* (1947). Maddow had made his reputation first as a pre-war documentary filmmaker and then later as a screenwriter, adapting William Faulkner's novel *Intruder in the Dust* for the screen in 1949 and then scripting John Huston's *The Asphalt Jungle* in 1950. Yet Maddow's name does not feature on the credits for *The Naked Jungle*, anymore than it does on other films of the period such as *High Noon*, *The Wild One* or *Johnny Guitar* to which he contributed. Blacklisted following post-war HUAC investigations, the writer was forced increasingly to work incognito. As with several other films (including *Johnny Guitar*), Maddow's writing credit for *The Naked Jungle* was given to his friend and fellow writer, Philip Yordan.

Regardless of the names on the credits, the filmmakers and their writing team faced a dilemma: Stephenson's short story was just that - a *short* story that would require significant expansion to reach an adequate running time. Not only this: 'Leiningen versus the Ants' was a robustly masculine yarn, featuring no female characters. (The women on Leiningen's estate are sent away as soon as it is known that the ants are drawing near: 'Critical situations first become crises,' observes a sombre Leiningen, 'when... women get excited.') Paramount were eager to dilute the testosterone and include a major female character. Their solution to both problems was to prefix the events of Stephenson's pithy action-adventure narrative with a lengthy prelude in which the dour Leiningen's world is turned upside down by the arrival in Brazil of his mail-order bride Joanna, recently married in New Orleans by proxy to the plantation owner and now determined to stand shoulder to shoulder with her husband in his Amazonian fastness.

Of a piece with this romantic realignment of the narrative was a significant change of title for Stephenson's

Eleanor Parker

yarn. In place of the blunt two-fisted challenge of 'Leiningen versus the Ants', the film's makers opted for the steamier and more provocative *The Naked Jungle* (one imagines that after his work on *The Asphalt Jungle*, Maddow in particular must have savoured the choice.) The late '40s and '50s saw the release of a slew of films with 'Naked' in their title (*The Naked City* in 1948, *Naked Alibi* in 1954 and *The Naked Street* in 1955 to name but three) as well as many that used 'Jungle' as a kind of titular shorthand for a general dangerous wildness, entirely regardless of the film's setting. The new title played down the stern heroics and ingenious engineering of the printed story in favour of suggestions of unbridled passion and romance.

The emphasis on romance meant other changes too. Where William Conrad's rich and velvety tones had been ideal for the 1940s' radio versions of the story, the stocky actor's portly physique and receding hairline were hardly the stuff of the Hollywood leading man and Conrad found himself demoted to playing the District Commissioner in the film. Leiningen's riding boots were filled instead by Charlton Heston. Still a few years away from his breakout leading roles in Cecil B De Mille's *The Ten Commandments* (1956) and William Wyler's *Ben-Hur* (1959), Heston was at the time best known for moody dramas and standard-issue westerns. Given *The Naked Jungle*'s melodramatic additions to Stephenson's storyline and the film's tale of rugged heroics in wild landscapes, Heston's film persona at the time made him all but perfect for the role of Leiningen. Certainly he is a commanding screen

Douglas Fowley, Charlton Heston, William Conrad

star in *The Naked Jungle*, towering over the others in the cast and holding the attention with his casual air of authority and brooding good looks.

Eleanor Parker, later known as 'the woman of a thousand faces' for her versatility as an actress, was cast as Joanna. Parker already had Oscar nominations under her belt for prison drama *Caged* (1950) and police procedural *Detective Story* (1951) and was arguably a bigger star than Heston at the time. Aged 31 and very beautiful, Parker had all the right qualities for portraying Leiningen's spirited yet sensitive new bride.

While publicity material for the film made it abundantly clear that its two leads would fall passionately in love before the end credits rolled, initially at least, the Leiningen's marriage is presented as a fraught one. Leiningen himself is cold and aloof, curtly rebuffing Joanna's affectionate overtures and taking every opportunity to avoid her company. The pair grow closer but Joanna's frustration with her situation deepens, and the script crackles with sharp exchanges between the newlyweds: 'I'm trying not to irritate you,' says Joanna with exasperation. 'I've noticed that,' retorts a sour Leiningen. 'I find it irritating.' Things come to a head when it transpires that Joanna has been married before. Dismissing her as 'used goods', Leiningen indicates that, like the piano he had bought to decorate his house, only the new and unsullied has real worth for him. Stung by Leiningen's prejudices regarding her previous husband, Joanna piquantly observes in possibly the film's best-known line, 'If you knew anything about music, you'd know that the best piano is one that has been played.'

So far, so stormily romantic. It comes as something of a jolt at about the 46-minute mark that the film abruptly changes tack and, with the lovers swiftly reconciled, segues into the events of Carl Stephenson's story. Conrad's District Commissioner announces the imminent arrival of the 'marabunta', or soldier ants. Tension and unease build as Leiningen, Joanna and the Commissioner travel up river to discover how close the ants have come. Discovering an eerily-deserted village, as well as the skeletal remains of fellow plantation owner Gruber, our heroes make plans to return to the plantation but not before - in one of the film's standout effects shots - they have seen the vast army of ants traversing the landscape: 'A flood of destruction. A monster twenty miles long and two miles wide. Forty square miles of agonizing death!'

It could be said that these scare shots and the longer climactic sequences depicting the final pitched battle between Leiningen and his

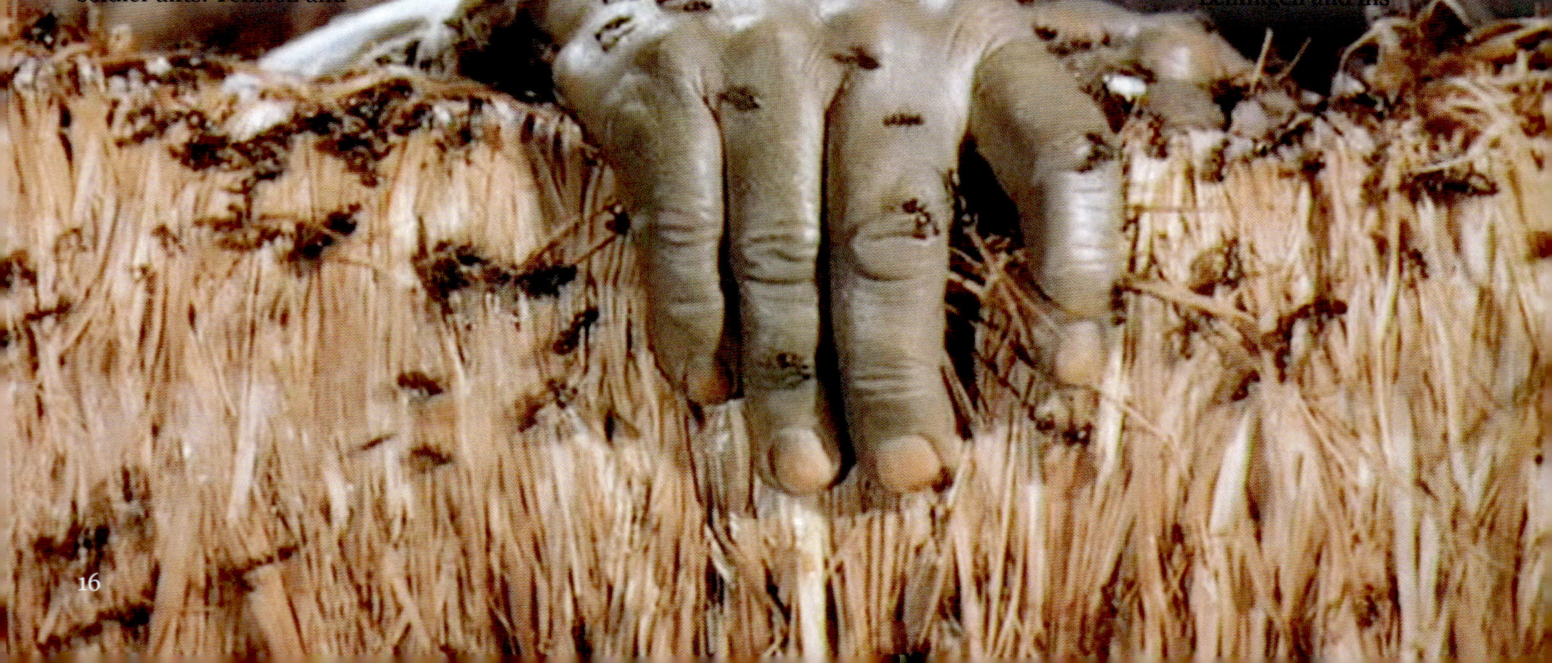

men against the ants position *The Naked Jungle* as a kind of forerunner to the cycle of '50s 'big bug' movies that began in earnest with *Them!* in 1954 and which went on to include, among (many) others, *Tarantula!* (1955), *The Black Scorpion* (1956), *The Deadly Mantis* (1957) and *Earth Vs The Spider* (1958).

Of course *The Naked Jungle*'s ants are an entirely natural phenomenon, the only thing about them that is giant being the plague proportion of their numbers. There is certainly no hint of the atomic radiation or alien invasion plan that is central to many of the '50s giant insect films. Nevertheless, readings of these other 1950s' 'creature features' as sublimated expressions of American anxieties about the threat of Communism undoubtedly apply to *The Naked Jungle* too.

The Leiningen of Carl Stephenson's tale may be a German, but Charlton Heston's Christopher Leiningen (he never gets a first name in the story) is emphatically American, dressing in the evening like a Louisiana gentleman and discoursing with Joanna on his family back home in New Orleans. Brazil may be a long way from New Orleans, but in the 1950s, Central and South America were seen by the US as strategically vital bulwarks against the spread of international Communism. In 1948, The Organisation of American States was created with the explicit purpose of fighting Communism's growth in the Americas. Its first signal success was the 1954 overthrow of the leftist Guatemalan government by US-backed forces. Much the same was to happen in Leiningen's Brazil in 1964.

The jungle terrain over which Leiningen conducts his war against the faceless invading horde must in other ways have felt topical for American audiences in 1954, too. The Korean War - some of it fought in landscapes strikingly similar to those of Leiningen's estate - had ended in ceasefire shortly before the cameras began rolling on the film. The way the ants are described ('They're organised. They are a trained army. They're not individuals. They have generals and they think. They actually think...') makes them sound less like insects and more like the kind of Communist-backed war machine that US troops had just helped bring to a standstill at the 38th Parallel.

As in Korea, Leiningen the American must lead the resistance against the encroaching enemy at least in part through paternal but rigid direction of the local population. The local populace in *The Naked Jungle's* case (portrayed on screen by an *ad hoc* mixture of Hispanic, American-Indian and white actors in blackface) is presented as credulous and primitive. In a key scene early in the film, Leiningen forces a shocked Joanna to witness a tribal ceremony in which a man is executed for adultery. 'Fifteen years ago they were savages,' says Leiningen. 'I took them out of the jungle. If I go, there'll be no civilisation.' It becomes clear that it will only be through the application of the American Leiningen's will and intellect that the marabunta will be beaten: as Charlton Heston rides ceaselessly along the lines exhorting his defenders to hold firm, various locals tasked with vital jobs either fall asleep at their post or run screaming for the trees as the ants approach.

It was a sight one could never forget. Over the range of hills, as far as the eye could see, crept a darkening hem, ever longer and broader, until the shadow spread across the slope from east to west, then downwards, downwards, uncannily swift, and all the green herbage of that wide vista was being mown as by a giant sickle, leaving only the vast moving shadow, extending, deepening, and moving rapidly nearer.

When Leiningen's men, behind their barrier of water, perceived the approach of the long-expected foe, they gave vent to their suspense in screams and imprecations. But as the distance began to lessen between the 'sons of hell' and the water ditch, they relapsed into silence. Before the advance of that awe-inspiring throng, their belief in the powers of the boss began to steadily dwindle.

Even Leiningen himself, who had ridden up just in time to restore their loss of heart by a display of unshakable calm, even he could not free himself from a qualm of malaise. Yonder were thousands of millions of voracious jaws bearing down upon him and only a suddenly insignificant, narrow ditch lay between him and his men and being gnawed to the bones 'before you can spit three times'...

--Carl Stephenson, 'Leiningen Versus the Ants' (1937)

The Naked Jungle remains a curiously disjointed affair, essentially uncertain of its genre. The joins are all too visible between the original adventure story and its romantic prelude, leaving the viewer to feel that they have watched two entirely separate movies. Despite Pal and Haskin's undoubted skills, only a few of the special effects sequences of the ants marauding their way across the countryside are truly dramatic; most of the deaths occasioned by the ants occur off-screen or are cut away from at the last moment, leaving the movie too bloodless to be a 'terror picture' proper. The film's greatest strength is perhaps in its leading man. Watching *The Naked Jungle* on release in 1954, it must have been evident that great things lay ahead for Charlton Heston. He is a charismatic figure throughout and, while the action of *The Naked Jungle* itself provided little reason for him to dream of a Best Actor Oscar, the power that he was to bring to his Prince of Judah five years hence is already in evidence here.

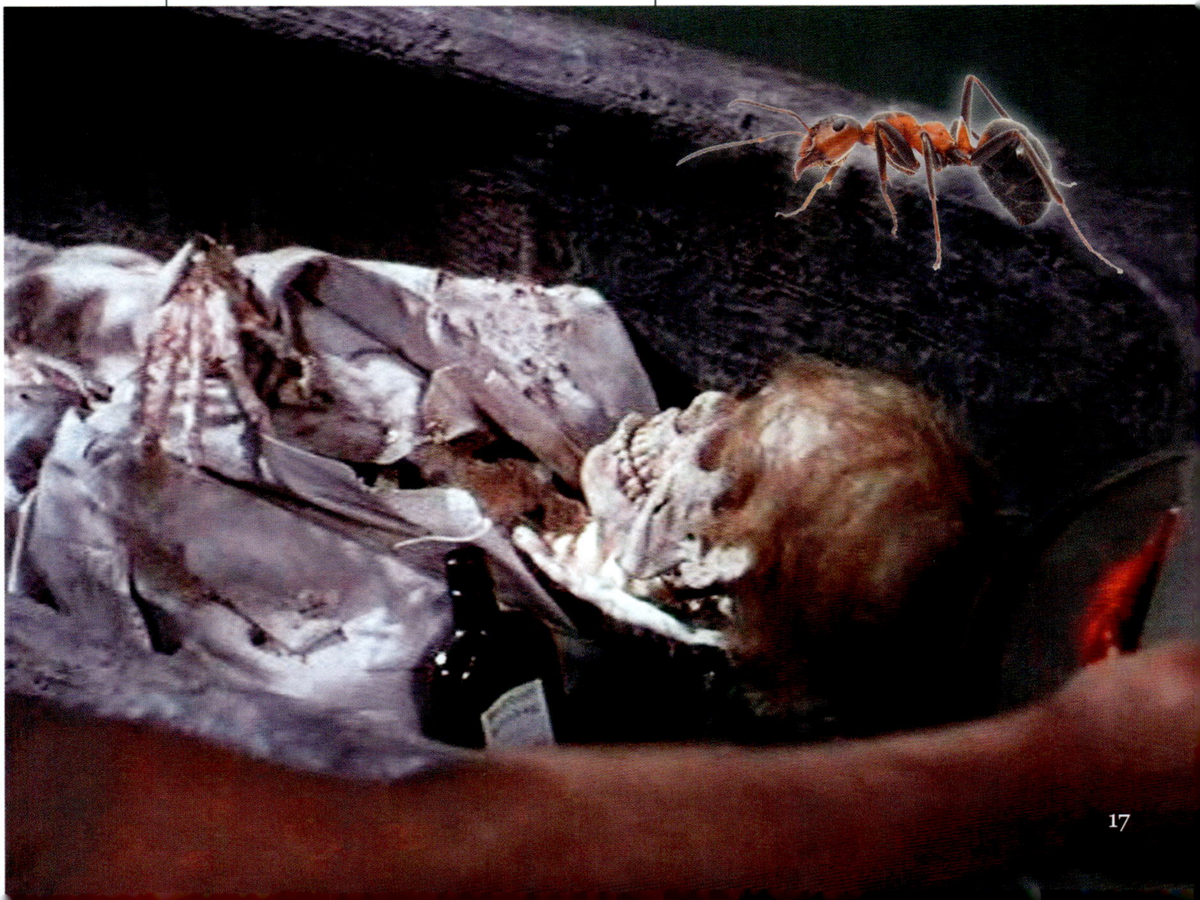

PEEPING TOM

Jonathan Rigby casts a cool eye over the outrage that greeted one of the most controversial British films ever...

'The immediate answer to trash like *Peeping Tom* is not more censorship, for that could only worsen a position rapidly growing impossible. The box-office is the real test... And that's where you come in - or rather, I hope, where you don't.'

--Derek Hill in Tribune, April 29, 1960

THE young Derek Hill was a regular contributor to publications as diverse as *Picturegoer*, *Sight & Sound*, the *Financial Times* and the left-wing weekly *Tribune*. In later years he would found London's New Cinema Club and its 1970s successor, the Essential Cinema, prior to becoming the first film buyer for Channel 4. But the progressive, sometimes censor-baiting nature of these endeavours sits oddly with his earlier involvement in the moral panic surrounding British horror films.

In 1958, for example, he had this to say when reviewing Terence Fisher's *The Revenge of Frankenstein*: 'The past months have seen the most relentless corruption of public taste the cinema has ever known.' Later the same year came an even niftier soundbite: 'Only a sick society could bear the hoardings, let alone the films.' But it was the April 1960 release of Michael Powell's *Peeping Tom* that inspired a line so quotable it even found its way into the director's autobiography. Hill concluded his *Tribune* review by frankly describing the film as 'trash' and urging his readers to vote with their feet and not go. But it was the baroque extravagance of his opening paragraph that hit hardest. It went like this:

'The only really satisfactory way to dispose of *Peeping Tom* would be to shovel it up and flush it swiftly down the nearest sewer. Even then the stench would remain.'

By April 29, when Hill's review came out, Michael Powell was already reeling from three weeks' worth of damning notices. They'd begun on the 7th, the day of the film's premiere at the Plaza in Piccadilly Circus, with Ivor Adams, in *The Star*, describing *Peeping Tom* as 'a film which, despite its brilliant technical skill, nauseated me.' The same day, Alexander Walker, newly installed critic of the *Evening Standard*, called it 'a clever but corrupt and empty exercise in shock tactics which displays a nervous fascination with the perversion it illustrates... Even brilliant colour photography by Otto Heller cannot reconcile me to a film as loathesome [sic] as this.'

According to Powell, the source of this disaster, which would ultimately pretty much derail his career, was a chance meeting at Shepperton Studios with the producer Daniel Angel, who had enjoyed a major hit in 1958 with the wartime drama *Carve Her Name With Pride*. Aware that Powell had recently parted company with his regular collaborator Emeric Pressburger, Angel recommended he work instead with Leo Marks, whose input on *Carve Her Name* had been essential, given his experience as an SOE cryptographer

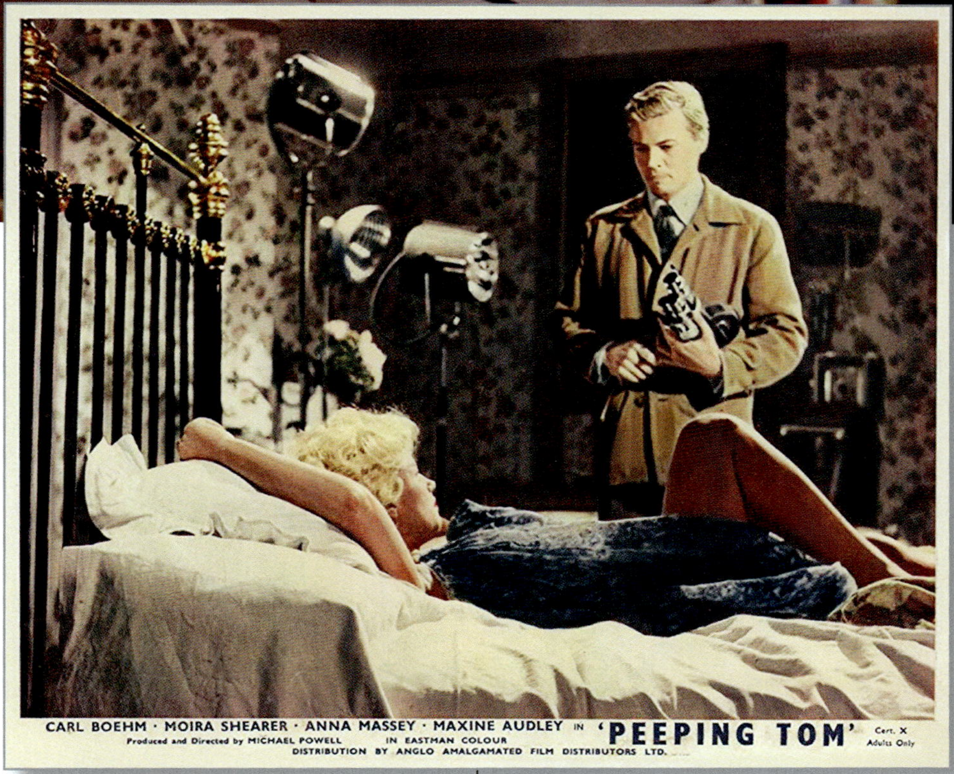

during the war. 'He's as crazy as you are,' Angel pointed out - and in no time at all, Marks was at Powell's Holland Park home, pitching various story ideas. The one Powell went for sprang from a simple but striking concept, expressed by Marks in the fateful formulation: 'Mr Powell, how would you like to make a film about a young man with a camera who kills the women that he photographs?'

'The script was written over a period of four to five months,' Powell claimed in 1980. 'Leo is a very slow worker, and I didn't hurry him.' For his part, Marks considered cryptography and psychoanalysis as natural stablemates - both of them involving the decoding of secrets - and recalled that 'Mickey's eyes were like a camera. They bored into me when I read the script to him.' The scenario that resulted concerns Mark Lewis (a name not a million miles removed from Leo Marks), a young film-studio focus puller who moonlights as a photographer of saucy pictures above a West End newsagents. Unknown to the naïve Helen Stephens, with whom he's conducting an extremely tentative romance, Mark is also in the habit of killing women with a blade concealed in his camera tripod, filming their death agonies as he does so. His illness is traced to his late father, a biologist who filmed Mark's entire childhood and subjected him to fear-inducing experiments.

Even from such a brief summary as that, it's clear that Powell and Marks were about to introduce the concept of 'snuff movies' to a startled world. Yet the National Film Finance Corporation apparently loved Marks's script, and the indifference of the Rank Organisation was quickly offset by Nat Cohen and Stuart Levy of Anglo Amalgamated, who arranged to co-finance the film with the NFFC. Cohen and Levy's embrace of the project was perhaps motivated by a film they'd sponsored in late 1958. Arthur Crabtree's *Horrors of the Black Museum* was a crude but spirited murder spree with an aroma of parochial sadism rather similar to what Powell was proposing. Not only that, in parallel with Powell's film, Anglo was sponsoring a third project in similar vein - Sidney Hayers's *Circus of Horrors*; in due course, critic David Pirie would bracket all three together as 'the Sadean trilogy'.

Powell's only major headaches in pre-production involved the unavailability of three of his chosen actors. Laurence Harvey had recently shot to prominence in Jack Clayton's *Room at the Top*, precipitating his move to Hollywood in September 1959 to star opposite John Wayne in *The Alamo*. This prevented him from playing, not only Mark Lewis, but also the dual leads in Terence Fisher's *The Two Faces of Dr Jekyll*. Two other actors were lost to Broadway. Pamela Brown, pencilled in for Helen's blind but insightful mother, was due to open in Bernard Shaw's *Heartbreak House* on October 18, while Natasha Parry, cast as Mark's second victim, was whisked away at the last minute when Odile Versois was dropped from Jean Anouilh's *The Fighting Cock*, scheduled to open on December 8. The director was Parry's husband Peter Brook, who cajoled Powell into relinquishing her in the course of a transatlantic phone call.

To replace Parry, Powell hit upon the celebrated ballerina Moira Shearer, having worked with her to electrifying effect in the Powell-Pressburger classics *The Red Shoes* and *The Tales of Hoffmann*. For Helen's mother, he recalled Peter Brook's Stratford production of *Titus Andronicus* and cast Brook's Tamora - Maxine Audley. And for the lead, he chose the 31-year-

old Karlheinz Böhm, who had become a continental heart-throb as Kaiser Franz Joseph in Austria's lavishly romantic trio of *Sissi* films. Billed as Carl Boehm, he could identify quite closely with the Mark Lewis character, being the only son of a domineering father - the famous conductor Karl Böhm.

Powell maintained an office at Kensington's old Viking Studio in St Mary Abbot's Place, which was a short walk from his home and was at the time largely given over to live broadcasts of BBC TV's *Tonight* programme. There Powell not only held his *Peeping Tom* auditions and rehearsals but also staged the disturbing home movies that chronicled the small Mark's terrorisation by his monstrous father. Filming on these began on October 19, predating the official start of principal photography yet constituting a crucial feature of the completed film. And here Powell made a curious decision that would be deplored by several critics on the film's release. In *The Tatler*, for example, Elspeth Grant pointed out that 'Perhaps the most horrifying thing about it is that Mr Powell has cast himself as the evil father - and has made his own small son [Columba Powell] play the boy he terrifies into madness.'

It was also on October 19 that Jympson Harman alerted *Evening News* readers to Powell's upcoming film, quoting Powell to the effect that 'It's not a horror picture. I want to create a lot of justified sympathy for the hero'. (Why the creation of sympathy might be antithetical to a horror film he didn't explain.) Eight days later, a readthrough for the cast took place at the YWCA in Baker Street, then principal photography finally got underway at Pinewood Studios on Monday November 2. The film shared Pinewood's stages with another Anglo-sponsored title that began exactly a week later - Gerald Thomas's *Carry On Constable* - and a non-Anglo item, Basil Dearden's *The League of Gentlemen*, which began on the 16th. By Christmas Eve, Powell and his team were sitting down to inspect the first rough assembly of the film.

In gnomic fashion, Powell observed in 1981 that *Peeping Tom* 'became a family affair and the family practically turned into a lens'. Underlining this family orientation, Powell cast not only his son but also assigned a one-line role to his teenage niece, Cornelia Frances. (She's given a typically peculiar Leo Marks double-entendre: 'I don't mind; might as well get pinched in a car as squeezed in a bus.') Powell also awarded the female lead, Helen Stephens, to the 22-year-old daughter of his old actor friend Raymond Massey. In July 1994, Anna Massey indicated that Powell's 'family affair' didn't necessarily imply on-set cosiness, telling Brian McFarlane that 'always, before a long and complicated take (which was presumably incredibly technical in itself), he had to have some sort of row, with a lot of tension going... He was quite complicated and not the most pleasant of men... It was as if he needed some sort of stimulus; it always happened just before a take that he would attack, so that you would do the scene with an added adrenaline'.

Interviewing Moira Shearer the same month, McFarlane was told something very similar. Having been offered the role of Viv at short notice and read the script overnight, she 'found it quite interesting, stupidly forgetting his sadistic streak'. Reflecting on all three of her Powell films, she pointed out that Powell 'was known as a bully, especially with women. Each day he would pick on someone, always someone in no position to stand up to him, and simply go on and on with cruel sarcasm until the victim was a wreck and unable to function properly'.

Leo Marks's script made much of London's burgeoning sex industry, beginning with Mark's murder of a prostitute living above Newman Passage, near Oxford Street, and then devoting plenty of space to his after-hours job as a glamour photographer. (The photographic studio is located above a corner newsagents in Rathbone Place; perhaps ironically, both Newman Passage and Rathbone Place are a stone's throw from the modern headquarters of the British Film Institute.) In painting a vivid picture of the coyly salacious world of late 1950s' pornography, Powell turned to the king and queen of that world, retaining the Soho photographer Harrison Marks as technical advisor and casting his business partner, Pamela Green, as Milly, the glamour model who becomes Mark's third victim.

In 1996, Green confirmed the Massey and Shearer accounts by claiming that Powell was 'a strange man, cold and somewhat remote, wielding a sarcastic tongue. His pastime appeared to be humiliating actors'. She also recalled his total indifference to the fact that his blistering camera set-ups gave her a nasty case of 'Klieg Eye'. More flatteringly, Powell's art department went out of its way to copy one of Green's self-designed photographic sets (a poster-choked Parisian street corner), and Green obliged Powell with the first - albeit fleeting - topless shot ever included in a mainstream British film. Underlining their authenticity, the beatnik-bearded photographic assistant in these scenes was played, uncredited, by Harrison Marks's own assistant.

Of the film's other main environments, Powell was clearly right at home in satirising the film industry. (Mark works at an obvious Pinewood clone called 'Chipperfield Studios', the name slyly suggesting that the film business is a circus, while the fictional film director is called Arthur Baden, echoing the founder of the Boy Scout movement - whose full surname was, of course, Baden-Powell.) And in a way, Powell was even more at home with Mark's domestic arrangements. Powell lived at 8 Melbury Road in

Kensington and used the house directly opposite - number 5 - for exterior shots of the residence Mark inherited from his baleful father.

Referring in part to Leo Marks's wartime eminence as a code-breaker, Powell would tell Jean-Pierre Bouyxou in 1973 that '*Peeping Tom* is, in a way, an entirely codified movie'. The signs and symbols - many of them black-hearted jokes - start up straight away, with the arrow-hitting-its-target logo, familiar from earlier Powell films, giving place to a screen-filling close-up of Mark's eye. The prostitute loitering on Rathbone Street is backed by a shop window crammed with dismembered female mannequins, and her approaching client is identified only through the several eyes of a whirring camera concealed in his duffel coat. On their way up to her room, he tosses something in a rubbish bin. A discarded packet of contraceptives, perhaps? No: an empty box of Kodak film. Then, in her cramped little room, the sharp-eyed viewer might notice a copy of *Picturegoer* on her bedside table just as the killer closes in.

Here, Powell picked up on the 'killer's POV' technique pioneered in such 1940s' Hollywood pictures as *The Lodger* and *The Spiral Staircase*, in the process providing a bridge from those titles to the slasher films of a later generation. 'Since any good director turns himself into a camera - *I Am a Camera* is the story of every director - I decided to do it that way,' Powell would tell Tony Williams in 1981. As it turned out, Powell's use of the killer's POV, not just as a dread-inducing trick but as a means of actually 'identifying' with the killer, was to be at the root of much of the disgust expressed by critics in 1960.

This riveting opening sets the tone for the whole film. The role of Dora the prostitute was, by her own account, offered to the 24-year-old French actress Mylène Demongeot, but, when her agent advised against it, it went to the 40-year-old Brenda Bruce - a much better choice given the dismal, dead-end milieu. The jaded, blank-eyed quality Bruce brings to a two-line role is truly memorable. When she first negotiates with her client (coming out with the film's classic opening line: 'It'll be two quid'), she twice cocks her head in a vaguely interrogative way - and, masterfully, she cocks her head a third time when faced by the initially confusing sight of the murder weapon. A murder weapon that we, the audience, won't get to see for 40 minutes or more.

Latterly, Powell would contradict himself over the film's darkly comic underpinnings, claiming in 1980 that 'There is no streak of humour running through the film, as there is in *Psycho*.' But, when writing his autobiography some eight years later, he called it 'a film full of humour and compassion.' Certainly it's hard to resist the hilarity of Miles Malleson's cameo as an elderly gent in search of 'views'. The pint-sized newsagent (Bartlett Mullins) gives them to him in a plain envelope marked 'Educational Books' and says to Mark, 'Well, *he* won't be doing the crossword tonight!'

And then there are the satirical pot-shots cunningly interwoven elsewhere. Michael Goodliffe's studio head is called Don Jarvis (echoing the Rank Organisation's despotic overseer, John Davis) and frets about 'what even a single day's delay would cost' with Viv lying dead in a trunk at his feet. Shirley Anne Field, who had been so wooden in *Horrors of the Black Museum*, was purposely cast as a copper-haired starlet who can't express

emotion, and the harassed film director trying to coax it out of her was entrusted to the one-eyed actor Esmond Knight. The film they're working on is called, ominously, *The Walls Are Closing In*, yet it appears to be a twee department-store farce, with Field's hapless fellow actor (Robert Crewdson) assuring the director that 'I'll keep it light'. Then there's the earnest young clapper-boy (John Chappell), who's keen 'to discuss that film at the Everyman' but also presents Mark with a saucy transparency. 'You don't get *that* in *Sight & Sound*,' he grins. Self-reflexively, the picture is of the real-life Pamela Green as her exotic alter-ego, Rita Landre.

Balancing this, in the photographic studio we get a grim disconnect between the truly intoxicating lushness of Otto Heller's imagery and the down-to-earth details of the models' lives. ('Can you fix it so the bruises don't show?' asks Milly.) More memorable still, the black-and-white home movies that chronicle the systematised child abuse to which Mark was subjected are profoundly disturbing, and greatly intensified by Brian Easdale's racing, silent movie-style piano music. (Powell's whispered words as the father - 'That will do, Mark; dry your eyes and stop being silly' - are as chilling as anything British horror has to offer.) And the secret laboratory in which Mark shows the films to Helen is sleekly modern yet also a grandly Gothic space worthy of Edgar Allan Poe, pulsating with reds and greens and even resonating to a dungeon-like drip-drip of photographic chemicals. Interestingly, this Gothic domain is situated in Mark's attic, contrasting with the subterranean cellar that harbours Norman Bates's shameful secrets in *Psycho*, the film Alfred Hitchcock was shooting in Hollywood at the same time - and to which *Peeping Tom*, inevitably, has always been compared.

It's in Mark's final scene with Helen, superbly orchestrated by Powell, that we're given the film's only glimpse of blood (it's Mark's own) and also the final sadistic twist - the revelation that Mark's 16mm camera, faithfully recording his unfinished 'documentary', isn't just fitted with a concealed bayonet but also a parabolic mirror. Which, of course, means that he doesn't just record his victim's deaths, he also records their fear and agony as they *witness* their deaths. Clearly, then, this grimly multi-layered narrative allowed Powell to give ultimate expression to his lifelong preoccupation with ways of seeing - a preoccupation that found its way even into the film's advertising, which depicted a hypnotically staring eye derived from a 1958 photograph by John Bignell.

'For some weeks an Eye has been staring out of newspapers and from buses; now, with *Peeping Tom* at the Plaza, it is upon us.' So wrote the *New Statesman* critic William Whitebait in April 1960, leading off a review entitled HOLD THE NOSE. '*Peeping Tom* stinks more than anything in British films since [Terence Fisher's] *The Stranglers of Bombay*,' he elaborated, claiming also that 'what worries me is that anyone at all could entertain this muck and give it commercial shape. The combination of the two is peculiarly nauseous'.

And on they came. In *The Spectator*, Isabel Quigly called Powell's latest 'the sickest and filthiest film I remember seeing' and

bemoaned the fact that 'all sorts of talented people have been used to hideous effect'. In the *Sunday Times*, Dilys Powell argued that her namesake 'did not write *Peeping Tom*; but he cannot wash his hands of responsibility for this essentially vicious film'. The normally genre-friendly Paul Dehn, in the *News Chronicle*, called the film 'amateurishly repellent' and a 'ponderous, paper-backed horror'. The *Daily Mail*'s Fred Majdalany dismissed it as 'a thoroughly nasty piece of horror non-comic by the gifted but wayward Michael Powell', while the *Sunday Dispatch* decried it as 'drivel', 'crude, unhealthy sensation at its worst' and a 'sickly mess'. 'As well as being as unpleasant as they come,' observed Campbell Dixon in the *Daily Telegraph*, 'the film is also silly, probability never being established,' concluding with: 'Sick minds will be highly stimulated.' And *The Tatler*'s Elspeth Grant began her review with: 'Mr Michael Powell's *Peeping Tom* is an exercise in sadism of which I cannot think without nausea.'

In the *Daily Express*, Derek Monsey maintained that 'As a shocker, it succeeds only in being nauseating for the sake of nausea. This is a sick film - sick and nasty'. Also in the *Express*, and returning yet again to that popular word 'nausea', Leonard Mosley confessed to 'a feeling of nausea and depression' while 'sitting through' the film and boldly asserted that Powell 'ought to be ashamed of himself'. In *The Observer*, CA Lejeune stated that 'It's a long time since a film disgusted me as much as *Peeping Tom*'. In the *Financial Times*, David Robinson claimed that '*Peeping Tom* is probably the first authentic British Sadiste film', but with the caveat that 'However intriguing psychologically, the film is frankly beastly'. And Nina Hibbin, in the *Daily Worker*, delivered the coup de grâce, heading her review simply UGH! 'I was shocked to the core,' she wrote, 'to find a director of his [Powell's] standing befouling the screen with such perverted nonsense... From its slumbering, mildly salacious beginning to its appallingly masochistic and depraved climax, it is wholly evil.'

The controversy was extended in late May when the Watch Committee in Reading, Berkshire, elected to ban the film (not having seen it), then in early June came some tabloid tutting over the film's new West End showcase at the Gala Royal in Marble Arch, the frontage of which was plastered with all the critics' most scandalised responses as a counterintuitive means of luring in customers.

Had Powell consulted the regional reviews, he might have been cheered by the anonymous critic of the *Middlesex County Times*, who enthusiastically equated the film with Franju's recently released *Les yeux sans visage* and said: 'Here is no Hammer-type horror. *Peeping Tom* is worth a peep.' But the prevailing tone was still largely negative. In the *Birmingham Daily Post*, for example, Keith Brace called it 'without question the most degrading film I have ever seen'. And when the picture hit Ireland in October, Martin Wallace of the *Belfast Telegraph* called it 'a sad, sick British film which deserves no place on a British screen', summarising it as a symptom, like 'the current rash of London striptease clubs and pornographic literature', of 'something rotten about latterday Britain'.

In the USA, the film was turned down by AIP (who had been more than happy to distribute its companion pictures, *Horrors of the Black Museum* and *Circus of Horrors*) and was finally dumped on the grindhouse circuit courtesy of the low-rent Astor Pictures. By the mid-1960s, the film was playing on US TV in truncated form as *Face of Fear*, after which the original version made its debut on British television, courtesy of Thames TV, on December 15, 1969. And by October 29, 1983, the BBC was ready to screen it for the first time, with *Radio Times* noting that 'This once controversial film is now regarded as a classic British film noir.'

Though the categorisation as film noir remains a head-scratcher, there was no doubt that by this time the film's rehabilitation was well underway. It was a process initiated in 1978 by Martin Scorsese, who had new prints struck and coupled *Peeping Tom* with Fellini's *8½* as 'the two great films that deal with the philosophy and the danger of film-making'. By the time of a UK re-release in 1994, at least one of the film's original critics saw fit to recant. Michael Powell having died four years earlier, the 93-year-old Dilys Powell announced that 'Today, I find I am convinced that it is a masterpiece. If in some afterlife conversation is permitted, I shall think it my duty to seek out Michael Powell and apologise.' She died the following year.

Alexander Walker, however, was having none of it, stating that 'I do not take back a word of what I wrote then' - and making a strong case for the real reason why the film had been so swiftly buried. The idea that the cause was a 'deluge of destructive but oddly undetailed' reviews from mere film critics he considered absurd; instead, he recalled a Variety Club event on April 12, 1960 (straight after the film's opening) at which he met Robert Clark, head of Associated British. 'We've put Nat [Cohen] in the doghouse until he gets rid of that piece of pornography,' Clark told him. Cohen, anxious for a knighthood that in the end he never got, was presumably only too eager to comply.

Whatever the reason, the reception accorded *Peeping Tom* in 1960 had a catastrophic effect. Carl Boehm, whose sensitive performance as Mark does so much to anchor the film, admitted in the 1990s that 'It was a deep, deep cut in my life. I hoped to become a big star and this destroyed my hopes.' Powell himself pointed out, in a gross understatement, that 'It did me a lot of harm professionally.' Even the inscrutable Leo Marks let slip, a few years before his death in 2001, that the film's critical drubbing 'broke my father's heart.'

Certainly the critics in 1960 were appalled by Powell's compassionate treatment of a psychopathic killer, an identification that reportedly extended to Powell dressing the character in his own clothes. ('Fear him,' rumbled Valentine Dyall in the film's trailer. 'But pity him also.') More than that, there was that superficially comic but actually rather troubling scene with an impish psychiatrist played by Martin Miller. 'Scoptophilia,' he tells Mark helpfully, is 'the morbid urge to gaze' - and in *Peeping Tom* everybody's doing it. Even the stolid cop on the case, played by the ubiquitous Jack Watson, is torn away from a football match on the telly to deal with Mark's final outburst. The film's complex web of voyeuristic references very quickly reaches out to entangle the audience itself - the viewers - who wouldn't be watching the film at all if they didn't share Mark's interest in violent and sexy spectacles at least a bit.

No wonder the critics were outraged. Their whole lives were spent morbidly gazing.

COVER GIRL KILLER

Martin Dallard frequents the back streets of Soho and finds a sordid world of men's mags and clip-joints, where Harold Steptoe tries to disguise the fact that his dad wasn't the only 'dirty old man' in the family...

Christina Gregg

Harry H Corbett

DURING the 1950s, the cinemagoing taste for all things dark and creepy had veered away from the classic movie monster. Instead, it gravitated to creatures from beyond the stars as the space race got underway. But audiences are fickle and as the 'Swinging Sixties' beckoned, so that taste changed again to something more real, and closer to home. The dying days of the 1950s brought about a new kind of monster - one that could live right next door to any of us: the serial killer.

Fledgling film producer Jack Parsons, later known for the likes of *The Earth Dies Screaming* (1964) and *The Curse of the Fly* (1965) dipped his toes into these murky waters with his 1959 outing, *Cover Girl Killer*. Released in September of that year, *Cover Girl Killer* was directed by Terry Bishop, who had started out as a documentary maker and is mostly known for his television work in *The Adventures of Robin Hood* (1956-60) and *Danger Man* (1960-61). Bishop also wrote the script, turning in a wordy narrative that attempted to lift the veil on psychosis and let the viewer in on what makes a disturbed individual tick. The 2nd unit director was Peter Yates, who went on to forge a stellar career as a director in his own right but also began on such fare as *Danger Man* for television, while the cinematography was handled by Gerald Gibbs, an industry veteran, whose career went back to 1933; Gibbs's more recent work included *X the Unknown* (1956) and *Quatermass 2* (1957) - both for Hammer - as well as *Blue Murder at St Trinians* (1957).

Cover Girl Killer was shot at the tiny Walton Studios, formerly Nettlefield Studios, in Surrey, with locations in London at the Serpentine Lido in Hyde Park and exteriors around St Anne's Court and Wardour Street. The film was distributed by Eros, a company run by

Philip, Sydney and Michael Hyams, which ironically had been making something of a name for itself by releasing exactly the kind of exploitation material that the killer in the story rails against - *Blood of the Vampire* (1958) and *Jack the Ripper* (1959) being typical examples.

The 'Cover Girl Killer' himself is an unnamed right-wing reactionary who sees it as his mission to 'clean up the streets' long before the Yorkshire Ripper actually tried it for real: 'Are we living in a land where sex and horror are the new gods?' he asks at one point, while providing both for a voyeuristic audience as Eros had its cake and ate it. The setting is the darkened backstreets of 1950s London, in particular Soho - home to smoky coffee houses and seedy nightclubs. One such club is The Kasbah, which becomes the hunting-ground for the killer, an 'ordinary' man scandalised by the tawdry nightlife that teems there and that has spilled onto the covers of the grubby magazines that can now be found in newsagents on local high streets. This anonymous avenger is played by Harry H Corbett, years before fame found him in the guise of rag-and-bone man Harold Steptoe in the BBC sitcom 'Steptoe & Son'. Operating under the assumed name of name Spendoza, and sporting a wig that looks like road-kill and spectacles better suited to Mr Magoo, he carries out his vendetta with military precision, his identity a secret for the whole of the film to maintain the notion that he is reflective of 'Everyman' - a mythical creature of Middle England, trying to uphold its values in a world rapidly descending into immorality and licentiousness.

Produced as a B-movie killer-thriller and running for a taut 61 minutes, this potboiler had to hit the ground running, and that it does as its crazed (or is he?) killer is already loose on the streets, dispatching the scantily-clad models who adorn the covers of pin-up mags with aplomb and a neat sense of macabre design: he even leaves his victims in the same pose that they had struck on the covers of the magazines that he detests, thus his nickname, and wearing the same scanty attire. When the police realise that they have a serial killer on their hands, they plan to trap the culprit with the help of Johnny Mason (played by the incongruously-named Spencer Teakle), an archaeologist by profession but now the owner of the racy 'Wow!' magazine, which he has inherited from a late uncle but which also happens to be the periodical whose covers have depicted every victim to date. With Johnny's girlfriend having been persuaded to act as both a model and the bait to lure the killer into the open, the trap is set. But will the pseudonymous Mr Spendoza fall for it?

In the meantime, convinced by his predatory promise of raising her profile, Gloria (Bernadette Milnes,) one of the Kasbah's burlesque dancers, has decided to see what the mysterious Spendoza - talent agent and supposed glamour photographer - has to offer. When he informs her that they'll be shooting into the night, with another photo-shoot at ten the next morning, the bubbly blonde announces, '10 o'clock? - I shall be dead!' How right she is, as she turns up on the banks of the Serpentine in a leopard-print bikini, and in the pose that she had adopted for the cover of the previous month's 'Wow!' - only this time, the rigidity in her stance is from rigor mortis! (Miss Milnes appears to have suffered for her art, as it looks from the film to have been a cold winter's morning and she must genuinely have been freezing to death!)

The cleverest part of the plot sees Spendoza assume yet another identity in order to book an act for the slaying through a theatrical agent named Lennie Ross (John Barrard). This he does to throw suspicion off himself and set up a red herring suspect for the bumbling police to follow. While giving details as to how, where and when the actor/patsy is to be at the specified time and place, we see him plotting a sort of film-within-a-film, mirroring exactly what is going on in the 'real world.' As it stands, you can't help but

Felicity Young, Harry H Corbett

sympathise with him, and let's face it - he's far more interesting to watch than the other characters on screen. But then what does that say about us?

The performances are pretty much as you'd expect for a film of this period - buttoned-up repression in tweed - and with its 'A' certification, the cinemagoers of 1959 already knew they wouldn't be getting too hot under the collar with the racy goings on up on the screen.

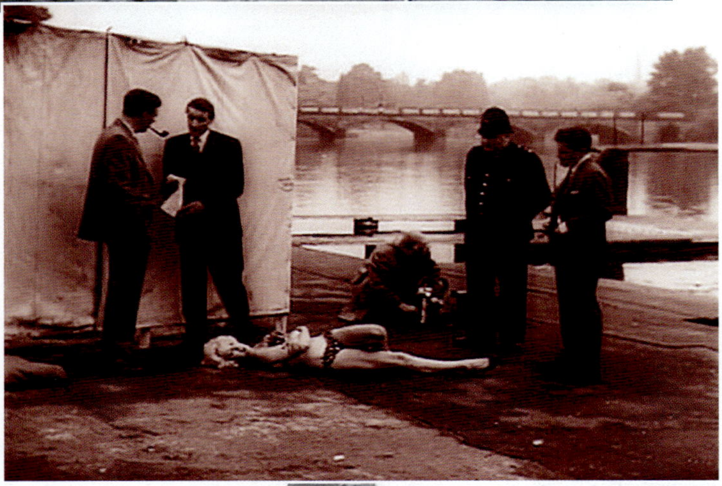

Born in Burma, his father being an officer in the army, Harry H Corbett moved to England when he was very young and later got the acting bug, joining a repertory company after his own stint in the army on National Service. The 'H' in his name was added early in his fledgling career to differentiate him from a certain 'Harry Corbett', the creator of the children's television puppet show, *Sooty*.

Corbett went on to appear in some two dozen or so films, the majority of them in a comedic vein after the die was cast for him as an actor when he became stereotyped as Harold Steptoe in the BBC's hugely successful Galton and Simpson sitcom in 1966. He never really made it on the big screen, and his most memorable role is probably that of DS Sidney Bung in Anglo's *Carry On Screaming* (1966), the 'Carry On' gang's homage to Hammer Horror. But it was the character of Harold Steptoe which clung to him like poison ivy and the two became inseparable in the public's mind, right up to Corbett's untimely death in 1982.

In *Cover Girl Killer*, however, he's not playing it for laughs, and he's clearly the best thing in the film. Even in the end credits we're not given the killer's real identity, and he's simply listed as 'The Man'. But we're introduced to him as Mr Spendoza, who passes himself off as a modelling agent-cum-manager, with photographic skills to boot. With the promise of lucrative shoots, and the possibility of more avenues opened to wealth and fame than they can shake a tassel at, the models are only too keen to meet up with Mr Spendoza, little realising that he has something altogether different waiting for them...

As well as Corbett heading the cast, there is Australian-born Spencer Teakle as Mason. Looking to raise the profile of 'Wow!' above more than just a skin mag, Mason poses as a cub reporter, which is why we find him at the Kasbah Club in the first place. Teakle first graced the screens in *Shall We Dance* (1937) then later in such outings as *The Gun Moll* (1953) and *First Man into Space* (1959), but he was best known for his television work in the likes of the BBC's Sunday-Night Theatre.

The object of Teakle's affections, and Corbett's main victim, is June Rawson, played by Felicity Young, who was primarily a TV actress. Young had only a few screen appearances under her belt

Bernadette Milnes

before this and she would go on to appear in TV soaps like *Emergency-Ward 10*.

Rounding out the cast is London-born Victor Brooks as Inspector Brunner. Brooks was always the reliable, straight-laced character actor and again best known for TV work such as *Z Cars*, *Department S* and *Raffles*; the two films that he would be best known for are *The Day of the Triffids* (1963) and *Goldfinger* (1964). In *Cover Girl Killer*, he is as reliable as ever, although he spends most of his screen-time quaffing large quantities of coffee and smoking a pipe. In-between boiling the kettle and lighting up, the by-the-book copper realsies that there may be a serial killer prowling the city, and his chief suspect becomes 'Wow!' owner, Johnny Mason.

The film is entertaining on several levels, its brisk pace glossing over all the inconsistencies in the plotting, and its game is raised considerably when the killer is on the prowl. Bishop keeps the tension ratcheted up in the last reel, with the showdown at the Kasbah notable for the fact that Davies's score is absent during the dramatic final moments, which gives the impression that the film itself is holding its breath while we await the fate(s) of Spendoza and June.

With its release in 1959 coming a whole year before the likes of Hitchcock's *Psycho* and Michael Powell's genuinely unnerving *Peeping Tom*, *Cover Girl Killer* could be said to be the film that introduced cinema audiences to the troubled psyche of the modern serial killer and paved the way for Powell and Hitch to explore the theme on a deeper level. But that would be stretching a point; Hitchcock had himself started the ball rolling with his *Shadow of a Doubt* in 1943.

In reality, *Cover Girl Killer* was a brisk, efficient second-feature which used its setting of Soho clip-joints as an exploitational come-on to tempt viewers away from their TV sets and back into the struggling cinema. Like many of its contemporaries, it promised more than it dared to show, with Spendoza's 'cover girl' victims barely appearing as though they'd had their thighs tweaked, let alone been molested and killed. Spendoza's motive is never really questioned, and he is given no back story to properly justify his actions; he is merely the threat that drives the plot to its sixth-reel conclusion.

Nevertheless, the film is interesting for the metaphor that Corbett creates of the Middle England backlash that was to overwhelm *Peeping Tom* only a year later, his 'Mr Spendoza' being almost a literal depiction of how liberal filmmakers like Terry Bishop must have imagined 'Angry of Tunbridge Wells' to actually look! Given the myopic views expressed in the press over *Peeping Tom*, it would seem that he was not far wrong.

Christina Gregg

REAR WINDOW

Barry Forshaw looks through James Stewart's binoculars and spots a murderer across the courtyard...

Be honest. You are looking across from your window at your neighbour's house, and you see them undressing. Do you instantly turn away or continue to watch furtively? If you replied 'I would immediately draw the curtain!', neither of Britain's greatest film directors - Alfred Hitchcock and Michael Powell - would have believed you. Both suggested that everyone's personality incorporated elements of voyeurism, and both made stunning films to prove the point. In Powell's *Peeping Tom* (1960), the very act of watching a film is a way of gazing at private, behind-closed-doors experiences - a notion that is also to be discovered in another masterpiece, Hitchcock's mesmerising 1954 classic *Rear Window*.

Many would argue that Leytonstone-born Alfred Hitchcock (1899–1980) is the most influential filmmaker that British cinema ever produced, in any genre. And looking at his British films (before his move to America and creation of such complex masterpieces as *Vertigo* (1958) and *Psycho* (1960)) remains a salutary experience. Early admirers who were not prepared to accept the director's own slightly disparaging assessment of his talents as simply the 'Master of Suspense' - notably French critics writing for *Cahiers du Cinéma* - prioritised the director's exuberant British films over his later American work, but that assessment has now been radically re-evaluated, with *Rear Window* near the top. And while the British films remain an astonishing body of work, brimming with a young man's fizzing intoxication with both his own talent and the medium he loved, from the early silent classics such as *The Lodger* in 1926 through the first British sound film, the innovative *Blackmail*, three years later, and up to the sublimely eccentric British version of *The Man Who Knew Too Much* (1934), Hitchcock's willingness to combine a playful attitude to the crime/thriller genre with a commitment to colourfully drawn characters and settings remains as winning today as when they were first made. Of course, these films, together with such vintage crowd-pleasers as *The 39 Steps* (1935) and *The Lady Vanishes* (1938), also began to explore the more complex and intriguing themes first identified by his more informed followers, notably the 'transference of guilt' between his characters, that would blossom after he crossed the Atlantic.

However, the sexual aspect of the director's works (notably the theme of voyeurism, as seen in *Psycho* and *Rear Window*) - not to mention his own personal behaviour - has come under the spotlight more recently, with his alleged

harassment of such actresses as 'Tippi' Hedren (something confirmed in this writer's conversation with her, though much disputed). This attention has led to accusations that there something is unacceptable not only about the man himself, but even about the dark sexual pathology of his films. Not, however, that this affects the director's genius one iota - post-Freudian explorations of the transgressive are a key element of twentieth-century film art. And although *Rear Window* is shot through with (unfulfilled) sexuality, the 'peeping Tom' aspects are more broad in application: the voyeurism of the central character, photographer LB 'Jeff' Jefferies (played by James Stewart), leads to threat rather than erotic release both for himself and for those around him. And, like Jeff, we are invited by Hitchcock to relish the sexual appeal of his fiancée Lisa Fremont, not least for the fact that she is played by the director's most iconic star, the exquisite Grace Kelly. The actress clearly embodied the kind of understated sexuality that Hitchcock favoured: as he put it to François Truffaut for the 1966 interview book *Hitchcock*, she was the cool, subtle 'drawing-room type' who was 'apt to get into a cab with you and, to your surprise, she'll probably pull a man's pants open'. Apart from her

Grace Kelly, James Stewart

Grace Kelly in a dress designed by Edith Head for *Rear Window*

Georgine Darcy

porcelain beauty,

Kelly always impressed Hitchcock by being totally unfazed by his dirty jokes (she claimed that she learned everything about sex from her days at a convent school).

In 1953, Hitchcock's formidable agent Lew Wasserman facilitated a multi-film deal for the director with Paramount (the five resulting films were *Rear Window*, *The Trouble with Harry* (1955), *The Man Who Knew Too Much* (the 1956 version), *Vertigo* and *Psycho*). The origins of *Rear Window* lay in a novella by a writer who (in his day) was regarded as something of a talented hack, but who is now seen as one of the principal writers of noir fiction, Cornell Woolrich. The story itself, which was written under the pseudonym 'William Irish', dated from 1942 and provided the basic plot for the film - but with none of the rich and complex psychology that Hitchcock and his screenwriter John Michael Hayes were to bring to the narrative. Most important was the fact that the central character was not to be presented as a standard heroic type, but as a man damaged in every sense whose consciousness moved in curious and difficult areas. The wheelchair-bound professional photographer Jefferies was to be played by Hitchcock regular James Stewart, from whom the director drew out more troubled psychological nuances than any filmmaker apart from Anthony Mann in Stewart's Westerns. Jefferies is incarcerated in a plaster cast after breaking his leg, and with the telephoto lens of his camera, he spends his time spying on his neighbours across the courtyard in which he lives. Moving beyond mere curiosity into obsession, Jeff studies the private mini-dramas played out under his gaze. But after watching a scantily-clad dancer among others, he begins to suspect that a middle-aged salesman, Thorwald (Raymond Burr), may have killed his nagging wife, and against their better judgment he draws into his suspicions his beguiling socialite girlfriend (Kelly)

and wisecracking nurse Stella (the sardonic Thelma Ritter). His actions are to place Lisa in danger when he sends her into Thorwald's apartment and watches, helpless, as the murder suspect unexpectedly returns. Finally - and inevitably - there is a fateful confrontation with Thorwald in Jefferies' own apartment. The premise of the plot - the half-observed murder with a witness who is not believed - is, of course, one of the most familiar in the history of the cinema, and one that has been homaged (or, if you prefer, ripped off) innumerable times in such books (and the subsequent films) - as Paula Hawkins' *The Girl on the Train* (2015) and *The Woman in the Window* (the 2018 novel by AJ Finn rather than the vintage Fritz Lang film from 1944).

The act of looking - or, more precisely, spying - is the key to understanding *Rear Window*, much as it was in the later *Psycho*, where we are put firmly in the position of Anthony Perkins spying through a hole in the wall on Janet Leigh removing her bra, and the director makes us utterly complicit in the central character's obsessions in both films. Who has ever looked away from these voyeuristic scenes?

Much has been made of the fact that the photographer's wheelchair from which the action is observed and (later) directed by the controlling Jefferies might be interpreted as the filmmaker's chair. The vignettes that Jefferies spies through his window resemble nothing so much as the cinema screen on which Hitchcock is presenting the action for us - and by watching the film, all of us become unwitting voyeurs (as with Michael Powell's homicidal young photographer Mark in *Peeping Tom,* where the opening murder sequence is shown entirely through Mark's viewfinder). There is an added charge from the sense of unfulfilled eroticism in the relationship between the desirable Kelly and the immobile Stewart as he watches with relish a

Raymond Burr

Thelma Ritter, James Stewart

nightgown being modelled for him. But there can be no sexual fulfilment because of his incapacity; however, despite the censorship restrictions in place in 1950s Hollywood, Hitchcock cannily lets us know just what is going on beneath the surface.

With his creative consultant Herbert Coleman and editor George Tomassini (as well as his reliable cinematographer Robert Burks, with whom he had worked in TV and who was later to perform the same invaluable function on *Psycho*), Hitchcock had in place his key collaborators. Not least among these was the talented screenwriter Hayes, with whom he worked on four consecutive films. As was so often his method, Hitchcock set himself a considerable technical challenge - something that he had enjoyed doing throughout his career to keep his creative juices flowing. Apart from the performances of his actors (who Hitchcock trusted implicitly to give everything that he required), there was to be the building of a massive and complex set, the construction of which was personally supervised by the director. The central character's Greenwich Village block of flats was designed as a set containing the 31 apartments that Jefferies can see from his window. Several of the apartments were completely furnished, as they simply could not have been lit properly in a genuine location. The results in the film speak for themselves - although *Rear Window* is undoubtedly a studio-bound film, Hitchcock makes a virtue of the fact; we are presented with a hermetically sealed, controlled world in which a variety of dramas take place - most importantly, the central plot strand of tracking down a possible murderer.

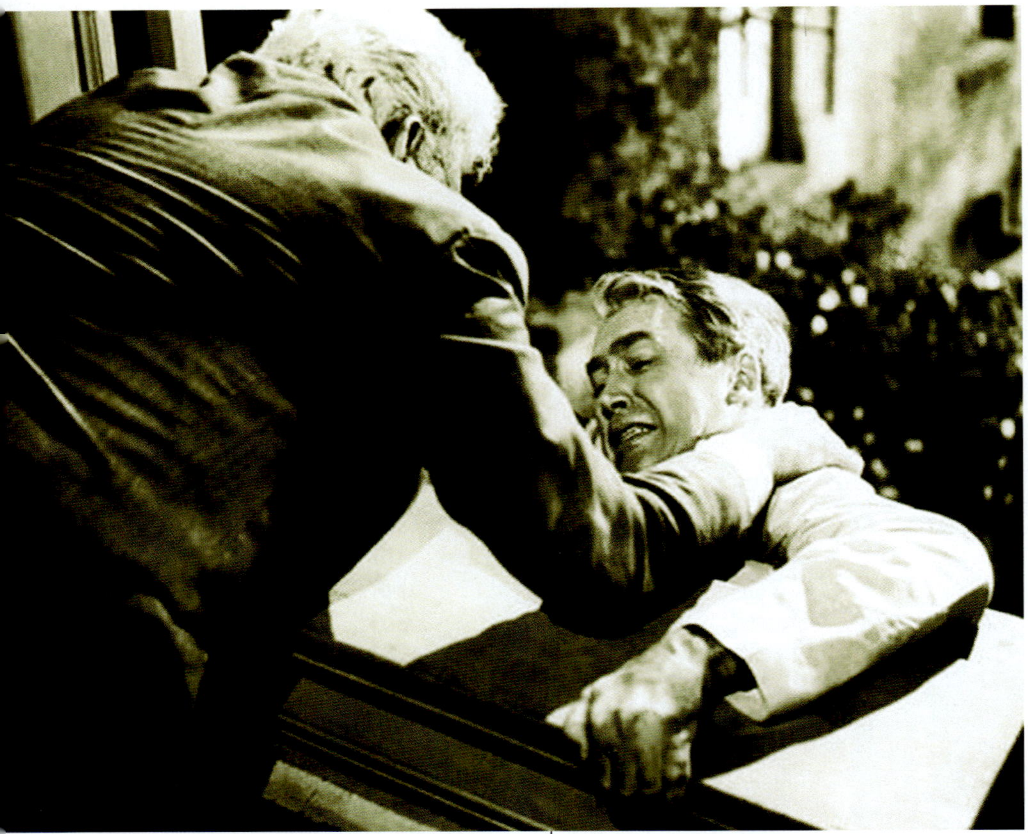

There is another insight we are granted by the film: how even in a crowded society where we all live cheek by jowl, we remain essentially solitary and alone. The various lives that Jefferies observes through his telephoto lens are not necessarily fulfilling ones - and his own certainly is not. The fact that he is unable to move from his wheelchair becomes a metaphor, suggesting how, like the neighbours he observes, Jeff is trapped in anonymity. And the fact that the film is open to such interpretations is further proof (if proof were needed) that Hitchcock is one of the most subtle and ambitious of directors in the history of the cinema, not just the simple entertainer he presented himself as. Far more than most of his peers, he holds the mirror up to nature and obliges us to look at ourselves on the screen - we may not be as glamorous or charismatic as James Stewart and Grace Kelly, but we are perfectly happy to accept them as our surrogates - and even to buy the idea that we are surrogates of them. We can also look at the various other neighbours on whom Jeff spies: a sculptress whose work shows a view of human nature as dark as that of the director and the character Jeff calls 'Miss Lonelyhearts', who may be about to commit suicide. What does the future hold for these other lives we have observed? The murderous Thorwald apart, all the characters in the film, from major to minor, are presented with the possibility of an improved, enhanced life, and this possible change of circumstance for them is set in motion by the 'unacceptable' voyeurism of the central character. So next time that you covertly look through a window at something private your neighbour is doing, perhaps you should not feel guilty about it. We are all - in the final analysis - gazing out of our own personal rear windows...

Alfred Hitchcock was famous for putting us, the viewers, on the side of his killers: the homosexual Bruno, for instance, in *Strangers on a Train* (1951) is a much more charming and charismatic personality than the rather conventional hero Guy, and Norman Bates' slightly awkward charm belies his dark secret. *Rear Window*, however, of necessity avoids this 'humanising the villain' approach, given that we are largely shown what the central characters are shown; the killer is seen at a distance, and although his culpability in a murder is kept from us for a while, it will come as little surprise even to first-time viewers of the film that the James Stewart character is correct in his assumptions - this is, after all, a Hitchcock film. But even with the strategy of keeping the murderer at arm's length, the director has a surprise up his sleeve when Thorwald finally erupts dangerously into the apartment of his tormentor. Counterintuitively, Hitchcock allows us to suddenly share Thorwald's vulnerability and confusion, asking why Jefferies - a total stranger - has focused on him and attempted to bring him down. We have been thinking through the film that he is a brutal and monstrous killer, but we are shown that he is a nervous and insecure individual - although still potentially lethal.

For a moment, we find ourselves briefly in sympathy with the killer (as in *Strangers on a Train*, when we are on the side of Bruno as he tries to retrieve a cigarette lighter in order to incriminate the hero - we want Bruno's fingers reaching down a drain to succeed in grasping the lighter). All of this is of a piece with the director's mischievous delight in incriminating us, his audience. Yes, Jefferies is a peeping Tom - but so are we all, Hitchcock persuades us, particularly when we decide that Jeff is correct in his suspicions. And society's disapproval and disdain for voyeurism is reflected in the attitudes of Jeff's girlfriend Lisa and cynical nurse Stella. Both women initially voice the expected criticism of what he is doing, but gradually they find themselves drawn into his obsessions and end up being equally voyeuristic in their pursuit of the truth. So strong is the film's persuasive power that, by the end, we no longer even view the spying as problematical but simply a tool for winkling out the truth. And if along the way we can put moral qualms aside - well, who is complaining?

BEHIND THE SCENES: Hitchcock directs

REAR WINDOW

TOP: *Alfred Hitchcock, James Stewart, Grace Kelly*
LEFT: *with Script Supervisor Irene Ives*
BOTTOM: *The Rear Window set in action*

GOLDEN AGE GODDESSES

Brian Robb looks back over the colourful life and Hollywood-royalty career of the first of 'Hitchcock's Blondes'...

GRACE Kelly's entire Hollywood career was confined to a few years in the 1950s. She made her screen debut at the start of the decade, and she brought her career to a halt just a few years before the decade ended, thanks to her fairy-tale marriage to Prince Rainier of Monaco. Kelly was born in Philadelphia on November 12, 1926, as Grace Patricia Kelly. Her eventual fate as an actual princess was not to a rags-to-riches story, however, as the Kelly family was already affluent. Her father, John B Kelly Sr was an Olympic athlete and triple-gold medal winner, who owned a brick manufacturing company. Kelly's mother was a physical education teacher and former competitive swimmer named Margaret Katherine Majer and had been a cover-girl model in her youth. With those healthy genes behind her, Grace Kelly clearly had a head start.

Kelly also had an 'in' to filmmaking thanks to her father's connections. His brother Walter was a vaudeville star who had switched to making movies for M-G-M and Paramount, while another brother, George, was a Pulitzer Prize-winning playwright who also drafted screenplays. With two uncles in picture-making, it was almost a foregone conclusion that Kelly would go to Hollywood.

While at school, Kelly followed in her mother's footsteps by taking up occasional modelling assignments at local social events (where she was joined by her two sisters, one older, one younger; Kelly also had an older brother). By the age of 12, in 1942, Kelly had won her first leading role in a play, 'Don't Feed the Animals'. She graduated in 1947, and the school Yearbook offered this 'prophecy' for Grace Kelly: 'a famous star of stage and screen'.

Her father John was disapproving of Kelly's decision to pursue acting as a serious career - it was, he said, 'a slim cut above a streetwalker'. Despite this, it was family influence that got Kelly started. She auditioned for the American Academy of Dramatic Arts in New York with a scene from her uncle George's play, 'The Torch-Bearers' (1923, and a 1939 movie). The Academy already had its quota for the season but Kelly scored an interview with the admissions officer, again through uncle George - it was enough to win her a place. She began her first term in October 1947, living in Manhattan's women-only Barbizon Hotel and working on modelling assignments to fund her theatrical education, making up to $400 per job.

It was to the stage that Kelly went first, winning a role in the Broadway production of Strindberg's 'The Father' alongside Raymond Massey. She played to good critical notices. Kelly graduated from the Academy at the age of just 19, performing the role of Tracy Lord in 'The Philadelphia Story' (which Katherine Hepburn had made famous on both stage and screen).

It was television rather than film that first brought Grace Kelly to the screen. She got her start in a trio of episodes for the Actors' Studio (1948-50), which adapted famous plays. One of her three roles was predictive: she played Princess Alexandra in an abridged version of Ferenc Molnár's 'The Swan', broadcast on June 9, 1950. These shows were the first of almost forty live television appearances, including on 'Somerset Maugham TV Theatre', 'Lights Out', 'Suspense', and 'Studio One in Hollywood', before her final TV role for Kraft Theatre in January 1954.

Country Girl (Grace Kelly)

BIG SCREEN QUEEN

Despite her television success, Grace Kelly's movie debut was low key. She scored a small role as a woman contemplating divorce in 1951's *Fourteen Hours*, a tense film *noir*. Kelly had won the part (on screen for just over two minutes) in competition with Anne Bancroft. Her photogenic appeal was noted by co-star Paul Douglas: 'In two senses, she did not have a bad side - you could film her from any angle, and she was one of the most un-temperamental people.' A visit to the set of *Fourteen Hours* by Gary Cooper gave Kelly's screen career a boost. She impressed Cooper as she was 'different from all these sexballs we've been seeing so much of'.

Gary Cooper, playing the conflicted town marshal in western *High Noon* (1952), needed someone who could play 'a young Quaker bride... suitably demure, vaguely Victorian'. He had found her in Kelly, but he had to persuade producer Stanley Kramer and director Fred Zinnemann. Kramer watched the actress in a play and decided to cast her despite being concerned about the age gap between her and Cooper; she was just 21 to his 50 (rumours persist of an on-set affair). Noted for its near 'real time' storytelling, in which Cooper's marshal awaits the arrival of a gang of killers with no help from the town he is defending,

High Noon (Grace Kelly)

High Noon was also a political parable of the McCarthy blacklist era (thanks to screenwriter Carl Foreman).

Cast as Amy Fowler Kane, Kelly lit up the screen in a demure bonnet. Zinnemann said of Kelly: 'She fitted the part admirably, perhaps because she was technically not quite ready for it, which made her rather tense and remote.' Released in the summer of 1952, the film scored four Academy Awards (for Cooper, editing, song, and score), and was unusual in that it climaxed with Kelly's 'rather mousy' (as Alfred Hitchcock had it) pacifist wife coming to the rescue of her husband. Kelly, however, was disappointed in her own acting, and while the film brought some attention (and is now one that she is primarily remembered for) it didn't make her a star. She returned to New York and took additional acting lessons. Of the finished film, Kelly said: 'I loved every minute of it, except when the wife was on the screen.'

JUNGLE FEVER

While neither *Fourteen Hours* nor *High Noon* launched Grace Kelly to instant stardom, an old screen test from 1950 played a larger role. Kelly had been up for a part in *Taxi* (1953) and although she tested well, she didn't succeed. Directors looking for new talent repeatedly requested the impressive test, but it wasn't until 1952 that Kelly's audition piece caught the eye of John Ford. As soon as he saw her, he reportedly declared: 'This dame has breeding, quality, and class!' Ford was in production on the romantic adventure *Mogambo*, and he cast Kelly as Linda Nordley, wife of Donald Sinden's David, on safari looking for gorillas. A romance develops between her and their guide Marswell (Clark Gable), upsetting 'Honey Bear' (Ava Gardner).

Mogambo would prove to be Kelly's breakthrough film - perhaps the fact it was made in Technicolor helped to show off her natural beauty in a way that previous monochrome films hadn't. The role came with a seven-year contract with M-G-M, with a relatively low (for Hollywood) salary of around $750 per week ($1500 was more the going rate). Kelly was happy to sign up but she had two requirements - she needed a break from films every two years to pursue the theatre, and she insisted on living in New York, not Los Angeles. But the studio would not entertain her third requirement - that she should be able to select her own roles.

Apart from the attraction of her fellow cast members and the opportunity to progress her career, there was another reason Kelly was keen to make Ford's film: '*Mogambo* had three things that interested me: John Ford, Clark Gable and a trip to Africa with expenses paid. If *Mogambo* had been made in Arizona, I wouldn't have done it.' The three-month shoot took in location work throughout Kenya, with studio filming near London. The movie was a financial success, making a profit in excess of $2 million, and it scored two significant nominations for Grace Kelly: a Golden Globe nomination and an Oscar nomination, both for Best Supporting Actress. *Newsweek*'s critic wrote: 'Her particular quality is the suggestion that she is well born without being arrogant, cultivated without being stuffy, and highly charged emotionally without being blatant.'

DIAL H FOR HITCHCOCK

Grace Kelly's best-remembered films are those directed by Alfred Hitchcock. In Kelly, Hitchcock found the 'trophy wife' he'd been looking for in his 1950s' movies. In a trio of films - *Dial M For Murder* (1954), *Rear Window* (1954) and *To Catch a Thief* (1955), Hitch came to rely on Kelly's icy blonde demeanour as 'the epitome of the femme fatale'. He had seen the same 1950 test that had so impressed John Ford, but he was waiting for the right film and the right role to utilise what he saw as Kelly's unique cinematic talents. He found both in *Dial M For Murder,* his film of the Frederick Knott hit stage play.

As Hitchcock was making the movie for Warner Bros, he required a 'loan out' by M-G-M to secure Kelly for the role of Margot Wendice, the wealthy socialite wife of retired tennis pro Tony (Ray Milland).

Alfred Hitchcock, Grace Kelly

Cary Grant, Grace Kelly

Margo is targeted for murder when her husband discovers her affair with crime writer Mark Halliday (Robert Cummings). Although shot in 3D (against Hitchcock's wishes), the film's release came towards the end of that 1950s' fad and prints were mostly shown 'flat'. Hitchcock said of the 3D process, 'It's a nine day wonder, and I came in on the ninth day'. Nevertheless, the dimensional version was one of the best of those that utilised the process, with Hitchcock's depth effects putting the viewer right on the set with Kelly, Milland, Cummings and creepy killer Anthony Dawson.

Hitchcock set out to give Kelly an onscreen 'sexual elegance', ensuring that she was dressed in a wardrobe befitting a character of her social stature and wealth, with her outfits changing to reflect her mood, from 'bright to sombre'. It was the beginning of an obsession for the director. He saw Kelly as a 'volcano covered in snow' and believed that casting her had saved the actress from a series of 'frigid' roles. Cursed with a host of social, sexual, and psychological anxieties, Hitchcock manifested his obsessions in his movies, striking a chord with audiences. His devotion to Kelly wasn't sexual, but he saw in her a woman he could mould into his 'ideal' - a cold figure with a burning centre of suppressed passion.

For one scene, where Kelly is attacked, Hitchcock took a full five days to film it, resulting in dramatic bruises. 'Mr Hitchcock often is reputed to hold actors in disdain,' said Kelly. 'But he actually has a special way with them, and is able to get exactly what he wants in the way of a performance. Of course, sometimes he merely wears them down until he gets what he wants.'

Kelly was willing to put up with Hitchcock's 'eccentricities', as she wanted to be challenged and wanted to take her career in directions that were not possible under M-G-M. For Hitchcock, it was Kelly's innate reserve, holding in a potential but rarely displayed sexuality, which made her perfect for *Dial M For Murder*. 'Actors often make the mistake of giving too much of themselves at the start and winding down.. Grace, as young as she was, had the ability to pace herself,' he said of his star, whom he nicknamed 'the snow princess'.

Kelly seemed able to cope with Hitchcock in a way that his other leading ladies could not because she was not wedded to Hollywood - she didn't need the income (a family trust fund saw to that). And as displayed by her willingness to cut her career short at the age of just 26, she was not thinking of it as a long term consideration. Unlike most of those subjected to Hitchcock's more extreme 'coaching', the little fat man amused Kelly. In Grace Kelly, Hitchcock had found his ideal blonde, and he wasn't about to let her go. She embodied the figure of the woman who withholds whatever it is the man is after - be it love, sex, adulation, respect or appreciation.

In *Rear Window*, Kelly was cast as the wife of incapacitated photographer James Stewart, who believes he has uncovered evidence of a murder in his Greenwich Village courtyard apartment. When the offer came through, Kelly had to make a choice between working with Hitchcock again or taking a role in *On the Waterfront* (1954). She went with Hitchcock, leaving the Elia Kazan film to Eva Marie Saint (who also later worked with Hitchcock). Several biographers believe Kelly took the role as it best reflected her true self, a character added to the film but not in the Cornell Woolrich short source story.

Her *Rear Window* co-star, James Stewart, recognised that Grace Kelly simply didn't need Hollywood, so was freer than most 1950s' actresses. 'By the time she reached here [Hollywood], she was a skilled and competent actress. She wasn't found behind a counter in a drugstore or luncheonette or at a drive-in. She didn't have to be nice to this guy or that guy to get ahead.'

Having been given an amazing build up by Stewart, who describes his fiancé as 'too perfect', Kelly gets the ideal entrance, waking the sleeping Stewart with a kiss - an image double printed by Hitchcock to emphasise its dream-like nature. Kelly's role as the 'dream woman' dressed to the nines, who would function as Stewart's avatar out in the world, investigating the clues to a murder, was simply perfect, finding her in the right 'mood' at the right time. Hitchcock's way of making movies allowed Kelly to be playful in a way in which working with other directors had not, hence her repeated returns to work with him.

LEAVING HOLLYWOOD BEHIND

Their third collaboration, *To Catch a Thief,* was filmed in the summer of 1954 in and around Cannes in France. It was a world in which Grace Kelly would shortly become very comfortable. For this romantic thriller, Kelly played opposite Cary Grant as the possessor of expensive jewels, who catches the attention of Grant's supposedly retired cat-burglar - is he back in action, or being mimicked by a new 'cat'? The David Dodge novel had been on Hitchcock's mind for a while as a potential film. Cary Grant said of Kelly that he had been impressed by her: 'Some people said Grace was just being herself. Well, that's the toughest thing to do if you're an actor, because if you're yourself, the audience feels as though that person is living and breathing, just being natural, not "acting" - and that's the hardest thing in the world to do.'

A lighter romantic caper film, *To Catch a Thief* reached the limits of what Hitchcock and Kelly could do together. Each film had brought the actress closer to simply playing herself on screen. In a pre-echo of her future, Kelly's Frances says of her and Grant's characters: 'Palaces are for royalty. We're just common people with a bank account.'

Hitchcock had discovered the essential 1950s' appeal of Grace Kelly - she was sexy and sexual without actively displaying it like Marilyn Monroe. In a discussion with French filmmaker Francois Truffaut, Hitchcock noted: 'Sex on the screen should be suspenseful. If sex is too blatant or obvious, there's no suspense. You know why I favour sophisticated blondes? Because without the element of surprise, the scene become meaningless. There's no possibility to discover sex.' In Grace Kelly, Hitchcock had 'discovered' sex.

The remainder of Grace Kelly's eleven films are not as well remembered as the trio of Hitchcock movies, but all have something that makes them worth watching, often simply Kelly herself. In *The Bridges at Toko-Ri* (1954), she was again playing the 'wife' to William Holden's jet fighter pilot in a tale of Korean war heroics. Perhaps 'spoiled' by her Hitchcock experiences, where she had enjoyed great input, Kelly found herself having a tough time with M-G-M, having been put on suspension several times for refusing roles. She wanted another loan out from M-G-M to star in *The Country Girl* (1954, from a Clifford Odets play), in order to play the unglamorous role of the downtrodden wife of an alcoholic actor and singer (Bing Crosby) attracted to his best friend (William Holden, again). When the studio refused to release her, the actress threatened to quit. Kelly saw potential in the against-type role (having read the play) that eluded those at M-G-M, and she would be vindicated by winning a Best Actress Oscar, beating Judy Garland, who had been considered the favourite for *A Star is Born* (1954) - Garland reportedly responded to Kelly's win with, 'I didn't appreciate Grace Kelly taking off her make-up and walking away with my Oscar'. The win made her M-G-M's most valuable star, but they simply didn't know how to exploit her. The largely forgotten mining drama *Green Fire* (1954) followed, with Kelly supporting Stewart Granger's treasure hunter in a role in a 10-day shoot that she had objected to and found to be an 'awful' experience.

MONACO BOUND

Grace Kelly came full circle at the end of her career with the role of Princess Alexandra in *The Swan* (1956), which she had played on TV in 1950, and her playing of Tracy Lord in *High Society* (1956), the musical remake of *The Philadelphia Story*, which had also been her graduation piece for the American Academy of Dramatic Arts. Both were predictions of the life about to come.

Kelly attended the 1955 Cannes film festival in France as head of the US delegation. One of her duties included a photo session at the Palace of Monaco with Prince Rainier III, ruler of the principality. Kelly struck up a relationship with Rainier. Having returned to the US to shoot *The Swan*, the relationship was largely a long-distance one through letters. In December 1955, Rainier was in America on a 'private tour', although there was press speculation that he was seeking a wife to fulfil a treaty obligation with France that stipulated if he did not produce an heir, the territory would revert to French control. During the trip, Rainier reconnected with, and proposed to, Grace Kelly. She accepted, and in *High Society*, she wore the engagement ring that he had given her. She had over four years left on her M-G-M contract and although she claimed she intended to continue to work, *High Society* was her final film. At the age of just 26, after only 11 films and six years in Hollywood, Grace Kelly was retiring. Ever the wag, Hitchcock greeted the news of the impending wedding with the statement that he was 'very happy that

Grace has found herself such a good part!'

Grace Kelly found her role as Princess of Monaco precluded her carrying on with her screen career. She had to turn down Hitchcock's offer of the title role in *Marnie* (1964) and her husband prevented her from taking a part in Herbert Ross's *The Turning Point* (1977). She narrated a documentary and a TV special, and worked with her husband on the 1979 30-minute short *Rearranged*, which was still in production when she died. Grace Kelly suffered a stroke in 1982 while driving on a mountain road in Monaco, losing control of her car. Her daughter Princess Stephanie survived, but Kelly died in hospital, aged just 52. Rainier did not remarry, and he was buried beside her after his own death in 2005.

Grace Kelly made few films, being far more prolific on television, but it is for *High Noon* and the trio of Hitchcock thrillers, as well as her final film *High Society*, that she is best remembered. She was a fashion icon of the 1950s and embodied a certain type of restrained, yet beautiful womanhood. She was largely in control of her own career, despite the efforts of M-G-M. As a result of her headstrong nature, she never indulged in any 'cheesecake' photography or B movie roles, as was expected of most 1950s' rising stars. She never played directly on her sexuality but as Hitchcock revealed, it was always there, simmering under the pristine surface.

At the end of January 1955, just as her film career was winding down, Grace Kelly appeared on the cover of *Time* magazine, which described her as one of the era's top movie stars, a figure who was 'a startling change from the run of smoky film sirens' Hollywood usually served up. Her ultimate fate, as real life royalty, seems to have been encoded in her film and TV career from the very beginning, where the idea of her as a Hollywood Princess was part and parcel of her screen persona.

Grace Kelly, Prince Rainier III of Monaco

THE KILLER IS LOOSE

Jim O'Brien finds Wendell Corey cast against type as a killer out to revenge himself on the cop he holds responsible for the death of his wife...

DESPITE having a short running time (barely 73 minutes elapse before the film's end credits roll), displaying an obviously spartan budget and having at its heart an essentially undemanding story about a convicted bank robber seeking to revenge himself on the cop who put him behind bars by hunting down and killing the latter's wife, director Budd Boetticher's 1956 crime drama nevertheless succeeds admirably where many similar films fail.

There's no doubt that the strong performances of the film's three leads are largely responsible for making of *The Killer is Loose* something more than the run-of-the-mill cop drama it might have been. Wendell Corey, fresh from appearances in Hitchcock's *Rear Window* (1954) and crime drama *The Big Knife* (1955), is chillingly good as the film's disturbingly mild-mannered yet psychopathic villain, Leon 'Foggy' Poole. Joseph Cotten was by 1956 no longer quite the A-list star who had earlier made *Citizen Kane*, *The Magnificent Ambersons*, *Journey into Fear* and *The Third Man* with or alongside Orson Welles, but he remained a big over-the-title 'name' and his performance as Poole's nemesis, clean-cut LAPD Detective Sam Wagner, is quietly effective. Rhonda Fleming (dubbed at the time 'the Queen of Technicolor' due to her scintillating red hair and shapely good looks) has perhaps the tougher job as Wagner's wife Lila, the object of Poole's murderous intentions. Dealing with a less-developed part than those of her male co-leads, Fleming still gives a strong performance both as the frightened target of Poole's obsession and as the bored housewife frustrated by playing second fiddle to her dedicated husband's police career.

Yet the film's three central actors aside, Boetticher's unflashy but solid direction also deserves credit for making what might otherwise have been a wholly middle-of-the-road crime yarn into something rarer and altogether more memorable. Tight the budget may have been, but Boetticher made good use of what he was given to work with; indeed, he was able in many ways to make a virtue of his financial restrictions, using his limited means to nurture a tauter and arguably more compelling narrative than might have come to pass had the available funds been greater. Thanks to cinematographer Lucien Ballard, *The Killer is Loose* also looks good, particularly in the sun-drenched opening sequence as the bank heist that sets off the film's chain of events unfolds, and then again in the movie's closing minutes, as storms lash the darkened streets of the LA suburbs.

In the savings-and-loans raid that opens the movie, armed raiders successfully make off with thousands of dollars in cash. Quiet bank clerk Leon Poole appears initially to have been a modest hero, having tackled the gunmen and been beaten to the floor for his pains. However, police enquiries reveal that Poole was an inside man on the job. In the scuffle to arrest him, Lieutenant Sam Wagner accidentally shoots dead Poole's young wife, Doris. Poole is sent down for ten years in the State Penitentiary for his part in the robbery but he vows revenge on Wagner and on his wife Lila. Transferred to a less austere prison farm as a reward for good behaviour, Poole makes his escape, killing first a prison guard and then a local farmer, whose truck and driving licence he steals. Armed with a gun following a break-in at a hardware store, Poole then heads back to the city, intent on killing Lila Wagner. Attempts to capture Poole en route are unsuccessful and the police decide to embark on the risky strategy of using Lila as bait in a trap that can be sprung on the killer once he arrives in town. The plan is to allow Poole to believe that Lila is home alone; in fact, Sam Wagner and other armed police will lie in wait for him while Lila is safe in the nearby home of Wagner's cop partner, Chris Gillespie. But having argued with her husband over his seemingly blind adherence to his job, Lila abandons the sanctuary of the Gillespies' house and heads home during a storm for a final confrontation, or reconciliation, with Sam. Poole, now clumsily disguised as a woman following the murder of his old army Sergeant Otto Flanders, stalks Lila as she walks alone through the deserted night-time streets. Just as Poole is about to strike, Sam, Gillespie and the other policemen hidden in the nearby houses shoot the killer down. He dies outstretched on the Wagners' front lawn while Lila and Sam kiss, their estrangement forgotten.

The Killer is Loose began life as a short story in the magazine *Saturday Evening Post* in June 1953, written by brothers John and Ward Hawkins. Boetticher and producer Robert L Jacks tasked screenwriter Harold Medford with converting the Hawkins's story into a finished script and shooting began at United Artists' Studios and on location in Los Angeles in the autumn of 1955. Boetticher had already established a solid reputation as a dependable director of B movies (no-nonsense westerns in particular, on both the cinema screen and TV, were to remain the director's chief area of expertise throughout his career) and he was able to bring on board an equally experienced and reliable cast for *The Killer is Loose*. Beyond Corey, Cotten and Fleming, the film boasts a fine set of character actors in supporting roles, with Michael Pate as Detective Gillespie, Alan Hale Jnr as LAPD beat cop Denny and John Larch as Poole's overbearing war-time army sergeant all delivering mostly unobtrusive but quiety convincing performances.

It has to be acknowledged, however, that *The Killer is Loose* never entirely shrugs off its identity as a quickly-made and unpretentious B production. The film's plot is riddled with the kind of bizarre coincidences and

Joseph Cotten

logical disconnects that could well have capsised the narrative. For example, no motivation is ever provided for Poole's participation in the bank robbery that opens the movie. Indeed, as the stick-up is depicted on screen, Poole's attack on the robbers seems entirely authentic and he is badly beaten, the hoods looking genuinely threatened by his impromptu 'have a go hero' moment. Also left unexplained is how the cops ever discovered that Poole was in on the raid.

Other plot contrivances could well have had contemporary audiences reaching for their coats: having already served a decent chunk of his prison time and knowing he is on the verge of early release for good behaviour, it seems bizarre that instead of waiting it out quietly on the Honor Farm and then exacting his revenge on Wagner without a full-scale manhunt to contend with, Poole busts out of jail in such a way as to guarantee that every policeman in the state of California will be looking for him as he attempts to reach Lila. Later in the film, we are asked to believe that the cops, having spent the whole day watching Lila like hawks, are nevertheless happy to leave her in the company only of Mary Gillespie and the latter's young son, even though Lila's potential killer is by then known to be close.

That such inconsistencies do not ultimately derail the movie is testimony to Budd Boetticher's skills as a director. The pace that Boetticher maintains is sufficient to hold audience attention throughout and whether scenes explaining plot-holes were lost on the cutting room floor or were simply never shot in the first place due to lack of time and money, the film builds enough narrative velocity in general to overcome any moments of weakness in the story's logic.

In some respects, ***The Killer is Loose*** actually benefits from not having all the scenes that might have been shot actually appear on screen: following Poole's escape from prison, several of the key incidents that audiences might have expected to see - Poole's murder of the farmer, which furnishes him with an escape vehicle; his acquisition of the gun that he will use to kill Lila Wagner; his eventual arrival back in LA - occur off-screen and are only made known to the viewer through other characters' dialogue. The effect of this is to make Poole's remorseless and cold-blooded pursuit of Lila all the more frightening for it being largely unseen and 'silent'. The viewer, like Lila, often doesn't know where Poole is or what he is doing - only that he is getting closer, and that he is serious about destroying his quarry. There is no hint of the supernatural about Poole as there is about Robert Mitchum's Harry Powell in *Night of the Hunter,* but the sense of remorseless pursuit is similar in both films.

Equally essential in building this notion of creeping dread is the depiction of Leon Poole as both entirely ordinary and at the same time dangerously violent - 'No ordinary killer', as the film's posters trumpeted. The film's first shot of Poole is from behind, as he deals, straight-backed and politely reticent, with an over-talkative customer in the bank. When he turns to the camera, we take in his suit and tie, sensibly side-parted hair and large, square-rimmed, milk bottle-bottomed glasses. Corey gives us a Poole who is every inch the quiet, nerdy nobody - softly spoken, slightly withdrawn, calm and collected. Yet soon this normality is shown to be disturbed. Poole's interactions with others are blank and emotionless. When Wagner shoots Doris Poole dead, her husband speaks to Sam in a detached, affect-less manner: 'I can't understand why you would do such a thing.. Don't you see how wrong it was to do that, to kill her?' Much later in the film, when Poole has invaded the Flanders' home, he talks with Grace Flanders in a similarly passionless way ('Please don't tell anyone, or I shall have to kill you.'), only to suddenly flare up into chilling rage when not brought food and a glass of milk quickly enough.

But Poole's 'disturbed ordinariness' is best caught by Corey and Boetticher in the final sequence of the film. Having killed Otto Flanders (exactly what he does with Grace is never revealed), Poole - still wearing his heavy men's specs and trousers - disguises himself in a ladies plaid overcoat several sizes too small, a rain hat, and a pair of women's wellington boots so as to be able to launch his assault on Lila undetected. The image is bizarre but powerful and is one of the highlights of the film. There is no suggestion of Norman Bates's later homicidal cross-dressing tendencies (and Harold Medford's script keeps any psychological pondering on Poole's motivations to a minimum) but the imagery is wonderfully unsettling. Corey's plodding gait ('There's something not right about her walk,' observes one of the police officers watching the approaching figure) and pantomime dame appearance are superbly contrasted with Rhonda Fleming's high heels and elegantly-belted trench coat as she walks nervously down the street ahead of her assailant.

That the cops don't see straightaway that there is something entirely wrong about the hulking 'lady' walking just ten paces behind Lila Wagner is pretty much of a piece with the movie's depiction of the police and of law enforcement officers in general. Whilst never becoming satirical (it is always clear that the police are the 'white hats', Poole the villain), the inadequacies of their response to Poole are a constant refrain in the movie. Early on in the film, Boetticher includes a scene in which the wiretap on the bank robbers is nearly ruined by the blundering actions of oafish, sandwich-scoffing beat-cop Denny, moments later, and Wagner's 'shoot first, ask questions later' entry into Poole's flat comes across as unnecessarily risky (in a way, Poole is quite *right* to blame Wagner rather than himself for his wife's death), and the warden at the State Pen and the overweight guards at the Honor Farm are evidently no good at spotting Poole's recidivist tendencies as they uniformly declare him to be no threat.

It is the clod-hopping Denny once again who blurts out to Lila that Poole is headed her way, having already killed several people. Boetticher then shows us a pair of traffic cops who, despite having had Poole's detailed description and photographs circulated to them (even this is played almost as police incompetence - the investigating team in LA obsess over phrenological interpretations of Poole's facial features and skull-shape to no very great end), cheerfully wave the murderer through their road block. In fact, the whole police plot to honey-trap Poole by (at least appearing to be) using Lila as bait to draw him out into the open is depicted as harebrained and highly dangerous. And in time-honoured last-reel style, the cops tasked with the stake-out on Poole are presented as poor-sighted, slow on the uptake and prone to potentially deadly indecisiveness.

No wonder, then, that Boetticher and Medford place a fair bit of emphasis in the film on Lila's disillusion at being married to a career cop like Sam Wagner. Although *The Killer is Loose* frames its female characters in ways that would have been entirely conventional in 1956 (Lila, Mary Gillespie and Grace Flanders are all presented as housewives and/or mothers exclusively), the film does give voice to Lila's frustration at Sam's commitment to the force, however dangerous the job may be. Mary Gillespie's too: 'It's a rotten business,' she agrees with Lila. 'It costs a lot and what does it pay?' Lila's isolation in a man's world is nicely caught towards the end of the film as she runs from the safety of the Gillespie's home to plead with Sam to reconsider his future. Boarding a bus in the pouring rain, Lila finds herself facing an entirely male group of passengers, all of whom initially stare blankly back at her. One of the men looks unnervingly like Poole and Lila recoils in fright from her macho surroundings.

Just a few years later, and Hitchcock was to take the cinematic depiction of a mild-mannered psychopathic killer to new heights with a film that makes *The Killer is Loose* look almost like a movie from a different century, rather than just a different decade. Yet Budd Boetticher's short short supporting feature very much deserves to be seen and enjoyed for the no-nonsense *noir* drama that it is. Wendell Corey's Leon Poole, in the tradition of Joseph Cotton's psychopathic 'Uncle Charlie' (from Hitchcock's suspense thriller of 1943, *Shadow of a Doubt*), is worth the price of admission alone.

Wendell Corey

KILLERS OF KILIMANJARO

Brian Robb goes on safari with Robert Taylor but finds the natives restless over his plan to bring cheap rail travel to the 'dark continent'...

Anne Aubrey, Robert Taylor

THE little-remembered *Killers of Kilimanjaro* (1959) concerns itself with the adventures of British engineer Robert Adamson (Robert Taylor) who sets out to construct a railway bridge in the African jungle after two of his colleagues have disappeared, presumed to have been the victims either of the restless natives or of the man-eating tigers that populate the area. The largely undistinguished director Richard Thorpe is perhaps best known as the original helmer of 1939's *The Wizard of Oz*, before he was briefly replaced by George Cukor and then Victor Fleming on what was a troubled production. The most interesting thing today about *Killers of Kilimanjaro* might be the back story to the production of the film rather than anything that actually ended up onscreen.

The melodramatically titled *Killers of Kilimanjaro* originated in a 1955 book entitled *African Bush Adventures*, co-written by JA Hunter and Daniel P Mannix. Hunter was a Scottish-born 'white hunter' who spent the better part of five decades leading safaris throughout what was then known as 'the dark continent'. He chronicled his adventures in several books, including *White Hunter* (1938), *Hunter* (1952), and *African Hunter* (1954) - note the prominence of that repeated word, both the author's name and occupation. He co-wrote *African Bush Adventures* (also known as *Tales of the African Frontier*) with Mannix, an American journalist and photographer whose 1967 novel *The Fox and the Hound* later became a Disney animated movie in 1981. Another of Mannix's non-fiction books was relied upon heavily by screenwriter David Franzoni when scripting Ridley Scott's *Gladiator* (2000). Mannix encountered Hunter when he, too, worked as a professional

hunter in Africa, sourcing wildlife for American zoos and circuses.

The film also drew upon another real-life story recounted in the book *The Man-Eaters of Tsavo* by swashbuckling hunter John Henry Patterson. Military man, big-game hunter and author, Irish-born Patterson's sense of adventure brought him to Tsavo in Kenya in 1898 where he supervised the construction of a railway bridge spanning a ravine. When the work was delayed by the threat of a pair of man-eating lions, Patterson - who had previously tangled with tigers - killed the animals over a three-week period, winning the admiration of the workers. The book charting his exploits inspired (in part) not only *Killers of Kilimanjaro* but also the films *Bwana Devil* (1952, notable as one of the first 3D productions), and the much later *The Ghost and the Darkness* (1996).

The story for the film was initially put together by Cyril Hume (science fiction classic *Forbidden Planet*; 1956) and Richard Maibaum (addiction drama *Bigger Than Life*; 1956; thirteen James Bond movies through to 1989's *Licence to Kill*). The screenplay, however, was written by John Gilling, who would become better known as a writer and director for Britain's Hammer Films. By the time *Killers of Kilimanjaro* came around, Gilling had been a screenwriter and director for over a decade. In the mid-1950s, he was associated with Warwick Film Productions, an independent British production company backed by Columbia Pictures. The founders of Warwick were Irving Allen and Albert R Broccoli (who would later go on to work with Maibaum on the Bond movies).

Warwick (named after a London hotel) was one of those 1950s' production companies created to take advantage of the Eady Levy (under which production qualified as British if it employed a majority of British technicians or actors) while at the same time using tax rules that allowed American stars to work abroad for a certain number of days per year tax free.

Warwick's plan was to make British films with American stars, but with international appeal. In a 1954 interview, Albert Broccoli confirmed: 'We're not making British pictures, but American pictures in Britain. Furthermore, we'll soon be shooting all over the world, bringing to the public the beauty and scope of the outdoors in new mediums - real backgrounds, but always with an American star.'

The star in question (at first) was Alan Ladd, who had quit Paramount in a dispute over money. Broccoli pounced, offering a three-picture contract with Warwick that also brought Ladd's preferred screenwriter Richard Maibaum along as part of the deal. They began with war film *The Red Beret* (1953) and followed up with *Hell Below Zero* (1954) and *The Black Knight* (1954). With $6 million in backing from Columbia and a British Government grant as part of the Empire Development Scheme, Warwick embarked upon a series of exotic adventure films made in British Commonwealth countries. Two films - *Safari* and *Odongo* - were shot in Kenya back-to-back in 1956, with *Odongo* being the first Warwick picture on which John Gilling worked, directing his own screenplay and featuring Rhonda Fleming in the lead role.

Odongo's tale of love between a white hunter (Macdonald Carey) and a vet (Fleming) in Kenya, made Gilling the natural screenwriter for *Killers of Kilimanjaro* (with the curious science fiction-horror-humour hybrid *The Gamma People*; 1956, crime flick *The Man Inside*; 1958, and *The Bandit of Zhobe*; 1959 in between for Warwick - Gilling was nothing if not productive). The natural lead for the film was Ladd, who had signed up for a further trio of Warwick pictures. He, though, quickly withdrew from the agreement, thus preventing his participation in the planned *The Man Inside*, *It's Always Four O'Clock* (an ultimately unmade adaptation of WR Burnett's *noir* novel), and *Killers of Kilimanjaro*. Journeyman

director Richard Thorpe (the vast number of his 180 films between 1924 and 1961 were for low-budget outfits like the poverty row studio Chesterfield Pictures) found himself without a lead for *Killers of Kilimanjaro*.

While Thorpe considered his leading man options, *The African Queen* (1951) screenwriter Peter Viertel helped out with revisions to Gilling's script in an uncredited capacity. (Viertel had chronicled his own adventures in making *The African Queen* in his semi-fictional 1953 account *White Hunter, Black Heart*, later filmed by Clint Eastwood.) *Killers of Kilimanjaro* already had former child actor Anthony Newley, a Warwick Films regular who had appeared in *The Cockleshell Heroes* (1955), *How to Murder a Rich Uncle* (1957) and *Idol On Parade* (1959), in the secondary, often-comedic supporting role of Hooky Hook. In the end, Thorpe felt that former M-G-M stalwart Robert Taylor was a decent enough stand-in for Ladd and made a nice contrast with Newley.

Nebraskan-born Taylor was the American film marquee star that Warwick Films needed for *Killers of Kilimanjaro*. His big break had come with 1935's *Magnificent Obsession*, but he had taken a break from such films as *Waterloo Road* (1940) and *Bataan* (1943) to serve in the United States Naval Air Corps as a flight instructor. Married to fellow film star Barbara Stanwyck between 1939 and 1951, Taylor was, by the 1950s, best known for a series of Westerns, such as *Many Rivers to Cross* (1955) and *The Law and Jake Wade* (1958). Out of his M-G-M contract by 1958, Taylor was a free agent endeavouring to establish his own production shingle with Robert Taylor Productions. On the cusp of the 1960s, when his film work slowed down and television took over, Taylor was only too happy to accept the lead in an exotic adventure film like Warwick's *Killers of Kilimanjaro*, especially as he had form working for director Richard Thorpe on such costume adventure dramas as *Ivanhoe* (1952) and *Knights of the Round Table*

(1953) for M-G-M-British.

Also in the cast was Newley's fellow Warwick contract actor Anne Aubrey as Jane Carlton, as well as make-up-the-numbers bad guys like Gregoire Aslan (as the caricature shifty Arab trader), Martin Boddey and Martin Benson, while the likes of Earl Cameron (102 years old as of August 2019), Harry Baird and Orlando Martins (as the Warush chieftan) had to make do with the rote roles available to British black actors at that time - African chiefs, assorted thugs and villains, and the thankless native roles. As with the treatment of these actors, the film did not engage with any of the issues facing countries like Kenya as the 1960s dawned - independence was still a couple of years off. The real-life chief of Chagga tribe, Thomas Marelle, happily took part in the making of the film but later complained about the change of title from the innocent-sounding *Adamson of Africa* to the more melodramatic *Killers of Kilimanjaro*.

Killers of Kilimanjaro was the 17th Warwick film that Columbia had financed and it was released at the start of November 1959. It had a preview screening at the Leicester Square Theatre in London a week earlier, but the critics were rather unimpressed. Regarding it as little more than a '*Boy's Own* adventure', the critic for the BFI's *Monthly Film Bulletin* said of the movie, 'Anyone who has a conscience about Africa will be appalled, [but] enthusiasts for screen slaughter should be amply entertained.' It was, they noted, 'a Western manqué of unusually hectic pace and antique morals.'

The film opened in the US on April 6 to similar mixed reviews. Trade paper *The Hollywood Reporter* said, 'Mixing of history and geography is acceptable when it serves dramatic purpose, but in *Killers of Kilimanjaro* it serves no purpose except to muddle what was originally a clean and straightforward story.' While the narrative was seen as muddled and incoherent (the railway is no nearer completion at the film's conclusion than it was at the start), some reviewers were able to appreciate *Killers of Kilimanjaro*'s big screen spectacle, especially as the film was presented in those 1950s' enhancements of Technicolor and Cinemascope, all the better to capture the lush wild landscapes, the resident wildlife and the expansive battle

scenes. The *Variety* critic noted that '*Killers of Kilimanjaro* doesn't go beating around "the bush" in search of a new dramatic path through Africa. It simply forges relentlessly down the same old cliché-infested trail travelled by so many past film safaris. Luckily, though, it's stripped for action, an approach that's never gone out of style at the box office.'

In attempting to appeal to the international, but primarily American, market, *Killers of Kilimanjaro* (and the other big Warwick productions of this period) played down their British origins (even to the extent of disparaging British characters or institutions) in favour of bigging up the Yanks. Basically this was expressed through the all-round heroism of Robert Taylor as the square-jawed, adventurous, but most importantly American leader of a bunch of British no-hopers. *Kinematograph Weekly* characterised these supporting roles, primarily that of Anthony Newly, as 'willing stooges' in the American's African adventure. Newly's Hooky is notably taken down a peg or two as he becomes comically entwined with various animal inhabitants of the African bush, including a group of charging rhinos and harassed hippos. He might get a brief heroic moment when he saves the kid Pasha (John Dimech, who later appeared in David Lean's *Lawrence of Arabia*; 1962), but he can't compete for the romantic attentions of Anne Aubrey's Jane.

Despite everything the film has going for it - the stunning locations, the local wildlife, a suitably tense soundtrack - *Killers of Kilimanjaro* is ultimately let down by an inadequate script, poorly deployed humour, and a dead-on-arrival romance. Aubrey, then just 22 years old against Taylor's 48, is simply dull and there is no sign of a romantic spark between her and her co-star - she fails to light up the Technicolor screen in the way that the leading women of the 1950s could. Born in 1937, Aubrey first appeared onscreen in *High Flight* (1957) at the age of 20. She was under contract to Warwick, and

appeared
in that flight school drama
opposite Newley, with whom she further appeared in other Warwick productions such as *Idle On Parade*, *The Bandit of Zhobe* and *Jazz Boat* (1960). At one time married to actor Derren Nesbit, Aubrey remarried businessman Peter Blatchley in 1975, after having quit acting with her final role in 1961's *Karolina Rijecka*.

The number of writers involved in drafting the screenplay is probably the reason that it doesn't really hold together, and the film overall plays as an episodic construction with no real narrative drive or direction. Even Robert Taylor sometimes seems just to be going through the motions, as if he realised while making the film that despite all it had going for it in terms of spectacle, *Killers of Kilimanjaro* would somehow add up to less than the sum of its diverse parts. The visuals are about all that save the film, but even they pale given the racial stereotypes and other 'superior' Western handicaps the
film fails to overcome. It is, however, an interesting failure, as buried somewhere in *Killers of Kilimanjaro*'s blithely colonial narrative is an anticipation of the 20th century conflicts to come in the sometime rivalries of the British and German companies involved in the exploitation of Africa, its resources and its peoples.

Perhaps *Killers of Kilimanjaro* is most interesting in its role as a precursor to the James Bond series. Shortly after the film was released, Warwick Film Productions was wound up following the failure of *The Trials of Oscar Wilde* (1960). Albert Broccoli, later better known by his nickname of 'Cubby', split from Warwick's Irving Allen to team up with Harry Saltzman in the creation of Eon Productions, which won the film rights to Ian Fleming's then little-regarded series of spy thrillers. And the rest is history...

Rod Labbe follows a trail of shrunken heads and finds screen vet Henry Daniell in possession of...

"THE FOUR SKULLS OF JONATHAN DRAKE"

I first saw *The Four Skulls of Jonathan Drake* (1959) during its original release and my overall reaction back then was 'meh,' followed by 'feh'. Sophisticated seven year-olds like myself, raised on blobs, cosmic monsters, Tinglers and sharp-clawed gill men, demanded more from their horror films than boring shrunken heads (hence the skulls), voodoo rites and curses, dank crypts, and a ghoulish zombie-man sporting sewn-together lips and a dour expression.

That said ghoul also wielded a jiggly rubber dagger and expired in puffs of smoke when his rump accidently met an open flame elicited yuks rather than shudders. It was almost like a Three Stooges routine, minus the loony sound effects!

Decades passed before I encountered *The Four Skulls of Jonathan Drake* again, objectively and maturely this time, paying close attention to important details. You know, the stuff kids, in their sweet naiveté, usually ignore: photography, art and costume design, musical score, acting, effects, make-up and plot.

Surely, this movie wasn't as bad as I remembered, right? Hmm.

And so, I purchased the DVD and popped it in, ready to relive a not-so-golden 'meh' childhood memory from my Baby Boomer youth and perhaps change perceptions and foster new opinions. The opening credits were certainly unnerving: a shadowy den or living room, and upon a cluttered desktop sits someone's skull and one flickering candle. Appropriately eerie music establishes the mood, telling me I'm watching a 'spooky' movie. Okay, I'm psyched; my seatbelt's definitely buckled!

WRITTEN, PRODUCED AND DIRECTED TO SCARE THE DAYLIGHTS OUT OF YOU!

Nearby, Jonathan Drake reposes languidly in an easy chair, his right hand clutching an ugly shrunken human head. He appears on the verge of either passing out or entering into a fugue state.

Atmosphere galore, and I had every reason to believe something creepy would soon happen. And guess what... it did.

Suddenly, three ghostly skulls materialise, bobbing and weaving. Are these the skulls of Jonathan Drake? Where's skull number four? Just as suddenly, they vanish. In walks Drake's daughter, Alison (Valerie French). She strikes a match, attempts to light the candleholder, realises her mistake, and successfully lights the candle. Poor Drake snaps back from swooning, and the stage is set for a nightmarish tale designed to frighten '50s' audiences out of their collective wits.

Horror and sci-fi movies from the '50s almost always 'enriched' their plots by inserting human drama, meaning laborious talk, scientific explanations, hand-wringing and romance, sandwiched between monster action and other frightful goings-on. Until the conclusion. At the conclusion, all stops are pulled out. We're face to face with whatever's menacing our heroes and heroines, and boom - the creature/monster/alien/psychopath

Paul Wexler

threatening life and limb is 'spectacularly' destroyed.

The Four Skulls of Jonathan Drake eschews the accepted template. Brief discussion enlightens us on murky plot points, true, but what's discussed proves essential. We understand that Drake fully believes his family, or at least its male side, are targets of a voodoo curse... each of them fated to expire at age 61, supposedly from heart failure. Heredity or mischief? Well, since this is a horror film, rest assured evil's afoot, reaching across the centuries to wreak sinister havoc.

Alison tells her father that Uncle Kenneth had called earlier about seeing a *tsantsa* (shrunken head). Uh-oh. Tsantsas mean big trouble; they're an omen, a sign of impending doom! Visibly shaken, Drake instructs Alison to wire his brother immediately - but it's already too late. Ken has spotted another tsantsa hanging outside the library window. Cue foreboding organ music!

Slowly, surreptitiously, someone sneaks in - a willowy, long-haired zombie-man bearing a sharp weapon and lips that have been sewn shut. Yeek! He dabs Ken's neck with the tip of his dagger, instantly incapacitating/killing him. Now, what must be done *will* be done: the ceremonial removal of Kenneth Drake's head for shrinking.

It's an opportunity missed. Rogers, devoted butler, enters, and the interloper beats a hasty retreat, job half-done (he'll return later to finish). Officially, Kenneth Drake has died from heart failure.. but we know otherwise. The Drake curse has claimed victim number three. And Jonathan is next!

What exactly is 'the curse'? It involves Captain Wilfred Drake, Drake's great grandfather, owner of a trading station on the upper Amazon. Because his Swiss agent had been captured by the Jivaro Indians, and they had 'taken his head,' Captain Drake ordered Jivaro men and 'man children' massacred.

The Jivaros are experts at shrinking heads, which haunts Great Grandpa Drake in a very big way. Though he had ordered all male Jivaros slaughtered, one fled.. an immortal witch-doctor possessing mad head-hunting and head-shrinking acumen.

Thus, a Jivaro death curse has trailed Jonathan Drake down through the Captain's lineage. Grandfather, father, his brother Ken, and soon, him. The victims all expire in their 61st year and are buried headless (stolen by that mysterious interloper). Later, the denuded skulls show up in the Drake family crypt...

An exciting premise for a horror film, at least on paper, but it's executed in such a clumsy and almost lackadaisical manner. Instead of creating an ambiance, we're let in on all the supernatural machinations right from the get-go.

Lurking in the background is one Dr Emil Zurich (Henry Daniell), a not-too-friendly 'friend of the family' who describes himself as 'an authority on Indian culture', specifically that of the Jivaro. Dr Zurich constantly wears gloves, speaks imperiously, and has other things on his mind than mere culture and archaeology. He and his undead voodoo servant, Zutai (Paul Wexler), orchestrated the slaying of Kenneth Drake and are carrying out the curse to its logical conclusion: the death, beheading and head-shrinking of Jonathan Drake.

This allows fourth-billed Daniell sufficient screen-time to chew the cinematic scenery, but identifying the villain so soon, and bringing us into his lab, shatters any and all built-up suspense. Blame the script for neutering what could have been an evocative mystery. This blunder is the film's greatest failing.

Henry Daniell had earned a solid film reputation, capably filling Dr Moriarty's shoes

opposite Sherlock Holmes (Basil Rathbone) in Universal's *The Woman in Green* (1945), but his two most memorable roles were as *Jane Eyre*'s (1944) nasty Mr Brocklehurst and 'Toddy' MacFarlane, making use of stolen cadavers in Val Lewton's *The Body Snatcher* (1945). Mr Brocklehurst, head of the depressingly chilling Lowood School (where young Jane is sent) orders Elizabeth Taylor's curls cut, snidely thwarts Jane (Peggy Ann Garner) at every turn, and runs the institution like an asylum. A classic characterisation.

An old pro, Daniell brings sobriety to *The Four Skulls of Jonathan Drake*, elevating its silly script and convincing us of his crazy obsession. There's no intentional comic relief; the tone is grim from first frame to the last, and Zurich's demise - while not spectacular - is very interestingly undertaken.

Really, I can't remember any movie more claustrophobic than *The Four Skulls of Jonathan Drake*. Not one shot is taken outside in natural sunlight. Several cars pull into driveways surrounded by imitation bushes and foliage. Walking from house to crypt encompasses traversing bogus landscapes dotted with 'trees' that have all the life of a store window display. This dead quality could have been foreboding and even dream-like (the fog-enshrouded forest in Lon Chaney's *The Wolf Man*, for example) but here, it's just stultifying. And chintzy.

One sequence does demonstrate a twisted morbidity, just what the witch doctor ordered. Like voyeurs, we're allowed a peek into Dr Zurich's lab as he 'processes' Kenneth Drake's decapitated head. Not a pretty sight and totally fascinating. How '50s' audiences must have swooned!

Alas, even experienced witch doctors aren't immune to mistakes. When Zurich pulls Drake's noggin from its basket, the lips are sewn shut. Next follows a prolonged process of boiling, filling the cavity with salt, and finally, shrinking. Once completed, Zurich sews Drake's lips closed.

Huh? *Two* rounds of stitching and sewing? Methinks someone fell asleep at the continuity switch!

Sans any mystery element, *The Four Skulls of Jonathan Drake* becomes a kind of race against time. Will Jonathan's skull eventually be added to the three of his brother, father and grandfather? And what about that stoic zombie with the dagger, shaggy haircut and sewn-up lips?

There will be answers. Officer Jeff Rowan, a local police lieutenant, arrives, fedora and 'all business' attitude firmly in place. He proceeds to interrogate Kenneth Drake's physician, the household butler, and meets a frosty Dr Zurich.

Rowan does little but blather, question, remove his fedora, take off on foot, fire a pistol, and squint thoughtfully. Since we're aware of Dr Zurich's nefarious plans, Rowan's sole real reason for being is to investigate why Drake's brother's head is missing and provide a little pseudo romance for Alison.

Nonetheless, *The Four Skulls of Jonathan Drake* moves along at a speedy clip. It is not long before Drake is also attacked by Zutai, and the butler fortunately interrupts and prevents a second decapitation. Drake is left paralysed and on the brink of death. Everyone but Dr Bradford, Ken's physician, thinks Jonathan is dying; he rightly deduces that poison brought on the paralysis. Except that this particular poison is not readily available north of the equator.

Could it be (gasp!) Amazonian?

Interest piqued (not always a good thing in horror movies), Bradford opts to confer with Dr Zurich, an 'expert' on Indian tribal customs, especially exotic poisons. Off he goes to the old doctor's gloomy mansion, where his unwelcomed curiosity buys him an impromptu beheading and head-shrinking. Ouch!

Henry Daniell

Eduard Franz

Officer Rowan investigates further and uncovers an entryway to Zurich's laboratory. There, an epic battle between Rowan and Zutai ensues. In the melee, Zutai's rubber dagger waggles comically back and forth, like a cheap Halloween prop. Imagine the howls of laughter when this played at Saturday afternoon matinees!

One hard push from Rowan, and Zutai stumbles back into the boiling pot used for head shrinking. Poof! Emitting a high-pitched yelp, he literally goes up in smoke.

The tables have turned. Zurich attempts a hasty retreat, but Rowan grabs him and tears away his collar. Do our eyes deceive us? He's actually an ancient Amazonian witch doctor with the head of a white man!

Ah-ha! So *that's* how the tribe's witch doctor escaped when Captain Drake's edict was issued: he had a white man's head sewn onto his native body! Gloves covered up the telltale hands. A shocking revelation and the only genuinely interesting thing about *The Four Skulls of Jonathan Drake*. Oh yeah, and let's not forget those head-shrinking lessons! Mighty useful tutorial.

Zurich keeps the prop people busy, sprinting past several feet of fake foliage until he is finally dispatched (his 'white man's head' severed from the 'brown body', as Drake explains) and he dissolves into a pile of ancient nothingness. He leaves behind 'the fourth skull' - his own. Everyone is happy, the Drake curse is lifted, and Valerie and Lieutenant Rowan share an embrace.

Edward L Cahn was an old hand at directing low-budget horror stuff, lensing minor drive-in fodder like *The She-Creature* (1956), *Voodoo Woman*, *Invasion of the Saucer Men* (both 1957), *It, the Terror From Beyond Space*, *Curse of the Faceless Man* (both 1958) and the underrated *Invisible Invaders* (1959 - a precursor to *Night of the Living Dead*); economy and speed were the trademarks of a Cahn film. In *The Four Skulls of Jonathan Drake*, he wastes little time on directorial flair. Why bother? - Just throw in a few uneasy scares and stick to the script.

Valerie French

Eduard Franz plays the titular Drake, someone I first thought collected skulls. What a surprise to learn otherwise! Today, Franz is best remembered for Howard Hawks's *The Thing from Another World* (1951) as Dr Stern, a minor character. His Drake is suitably anguished, even heroic, but he is not a very interesting individual.

Released by United Artists, *The Four Skulls of Jonathan Drake* was an independent Vogue Pictures production. It came just as the '50s' sci-fi/horror cycle in the US was reaching its end. Hammer and American International Pictures would soon dominate, as black-and-white programmers gave way to Technicolor, blood, violence and heaving bosoms. By comparison, *Jonathan Drake* is almost quaint - a reminder of old-fashioned chills, hot buttered popcorn, Coca-Cola and much-missed innocence. Sigh. We will never pass that way again.

The Naked World of HARRISON MARKS

Remember when you could go into Dixons and buy 8mm films by the cartload? Allan Bryce does, and he still has the cart. Here he shares his memories of Harrison Marks, who made hundreds of such glamour 'loops'...

Vivienne Warren, Harrison Marks

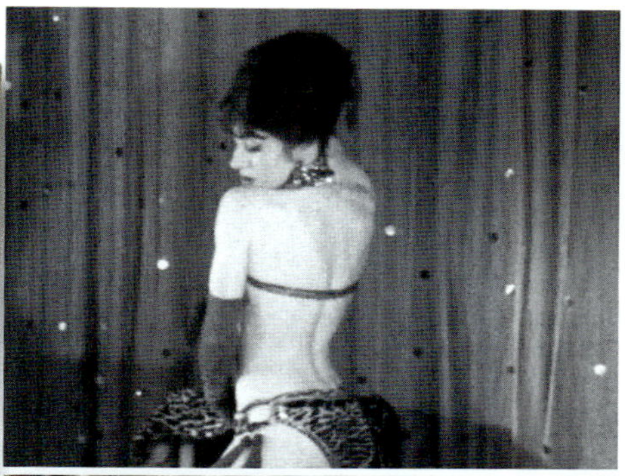

Burlesque Queen

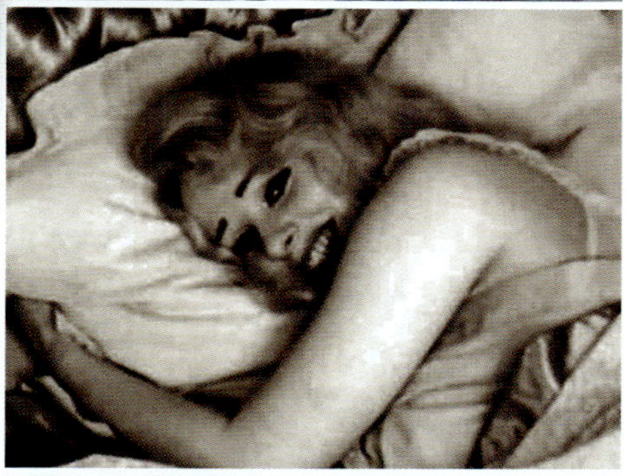

Goodnight with Sabrina

Long before the digital age, 8mm package movies were the reel deal, the only game in town for the committed film buff wanting to watch movies on a decent sized screen in the comfort of their own Armchair Odeon. Just under a quarter of the size of the 35mm films projected in the real picture palaces, Standard 8mm was developed by Eastman Kodak during the Great Depression and made its debut in 1932. A 50-foot spool lasted about 4 minutes, which wasn't long, though to be fair, Abraham Zapruder only needed 26.6 seconds of 8mm film to capture the assassination of John F Kennedy on November 22, 1963.

This new Bootlace Cinema allowed movie collectors to own drastically cut-down versions of classic movies. Laurel and Hardy and Charlie Chaplin shorts were good sellers but as with many new formats, the lure of adult material 'For Private Viewing Only' drove the market forward. Punters could also see short films in which women with unfeasibly large breasts exhibited them (or at least threatened to do so) for their educational viewing pleasure.

The market for such titles opened up in the late 1950s when ultra-soft romps such as *Goodnight With Sabrina* and *Burlesque Queen* were screened in between acts in Soho strip clubs. The former, out from Kensington-based Walton Films, promised, 'The most intimate film of Sabrina yet made, in which you see her slipping out of a glamorous evening gown into a silky negligee. Watch her revelling in the delights of a silky bubble bath - see her wearing the neatest nightie created - and finally wishing you a goodnight from the kind of bed that could only be Sabrina's! Actually filmed in her own luxury flat!'

Other Walton successes from these early days were *Paris Night Clubs* and *Bikini Clad Girls*, both of which were more about tassel-twirling tease than actual strip, despite the breathless descriptions on the 8mm boxes. But when glamour photographer (George) Harrison Marks - he dropped the George from his professional name - arrived on the scene with his very British nudie cuties, he raised the bar - and the bra - considerably.

It would be no exaggeration to say that Marks almost single-handedly introduced an entire generation of heterosexual males to their first sight of the undraped female form. When Marks launched *Kamera*, Britain's first nudie magazine, in 1957, it sold its initial print order of 15,000 within four days. Three months later, he was printing 240,000 at 2/6d a copy! Within three years he was a millionaire. He lost it all fairly quickly through drinking, womanising and ignoring letters from the tax man. 'I always had a lounge next to my studio,' Marks revealed. 'Come in, sit down and have a drink was always my attitude. To relax the models. And I drank too. Suddenly - bang, it was two and a half bottles of brandy a day.'

Back in the late

Sabrina

Harrison Marks

1950s and early 1960s though, George was on a roll. His enticingly voluptuous but airbrushed nudes also grinned back from within the pages of long-faded men's magazines like *Spick & Span* and *Parade*, and Bootlace Cinema fans could bring these dream girls to life on their bedroom wall by purchasing one of George's 50ft packages - available from Dixons high street retail branches everywhere!

These were no Hollywood epics. George's ladies were usually down to their birthday suits within half a dozen frames of the hastily superimposed title, and thereafter posed very coyly in the shower, bath or bedroom. Full frontals were out, so the lady in question would conspire to keep her legs crossed at all times - and whenever she stepped out of the bath there would inevitably be a fluffy bunny tail of soap suds obscuring the danger area!

I first met the great man, back in the late '80s, by which time he was running a spanking magazine called *Kane* and had cut his booze intake down to two bottles of Courvoisier a day.

He told me that he started out in vaudeville as a stand-up comedian, one half of an act called Harrison and Stuart, a teenage duo that appeared in variety halls in the late 1940s and early 1950s. 'It wasn't working, so I pulled out,' he said. 'I went on to have a very good training in the film business, working with a couple of wonderful cameramen who could do unbelievable things with lighting. And eventually I decided I wanted to be a theatrical photographer. So I opened my first studio in London in Gerrard Street, which is now Chinatown. Having been in the variety business, I had an intro to most of the agents around the area and before long, I must have photographed every top name in the variety business.'

His real breakthrough came through the popular funnyman Norman Wisdom, who was a close friend of George's. 'Norman was booked to star in the Folies Bergère at the Prince of Wales Theatre,' he explained. 'I had taken a picture of him, and when Bernard Delfont saw this picture he said, 'That's the picture we want to use for our campaign,' meaning it would be used all over London on big hoardings.

'He asked who took it, and Norman said, 'A friend of mine, a bloke called Harrison Marks, who takes most of the variety artists.' Delfont said, 'Well, get him on the phone and get him over here.'

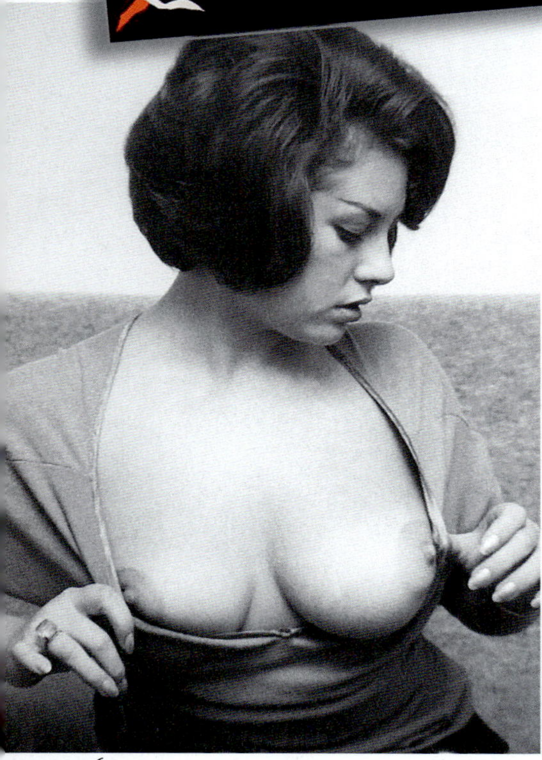

June Palmer / INSET: in costume for *Taste the Blood of Dracula* (1970)

At this point George smiled in reminiscence. 'It was very funny, because though I was photographing big names, there was only about fourpence ha'penny in it, you know? There was just about enough to make a living. I had some young kid who was working for me as head cook and bottle washer and every time the phone rang and he answered it, it was a standing joke that I'd say, "If that's Delfont, tell him I'm not interested".'

'One day the phone went and he said, "Quick - it's Delfont's office!" So I said, "Tell him I'm not interested." Then he said "It's REALLY Delfont's office!" And sure enough it was Norman Wisdom saying, "Get over here, I think I've got you the Folies Bergère!"

'Of course I was there like a shot. Cutting a long story short, Delfont looked at my stuff and said, "Yes, I like your work. How do you like photographing girls?"'

In retrospect that may seem a funny question, but at the time George hadn't had a lot of experience working with the female form.

'All my stuff was with people like Max Miller, Jimmy Durante, Jack Benny and so on. I think the only women I had done were Dorothy Squires, Ella Shields - who was 78 - and Elsie and Doris Waters, who must have been about 900. Basically, I photographed men. But Delfont still wanted me to have a go at the Follies, which was a big thing - a West End show. Suddenly I got landed with thirty beautiful birds, and I never looked back!'

Perhaps it was George's lack of experience at photographing women that enabled him to approach the subject with a fresh eye but, before long, the Harrison Marks technique had turned the glamour industry on its head. What did he do that was different?

Margaret Nolan in costume for *Goldfinger* (1964)

'I photographed them as I saw them,' he told me. 'It was a total revolution in nude photography. Up until that time, there were two or three very well-known guys who specialised in nude work. One was a bloke called Alan Duncan, and then there was John Everard and Walter Bird. All their stuff was like love-locked-out through a mist, but I photographed these girls as I saw them, with flesh and goose pimples - the lot. And within two years my name was known all over the world as THE man for photographing nudes.'

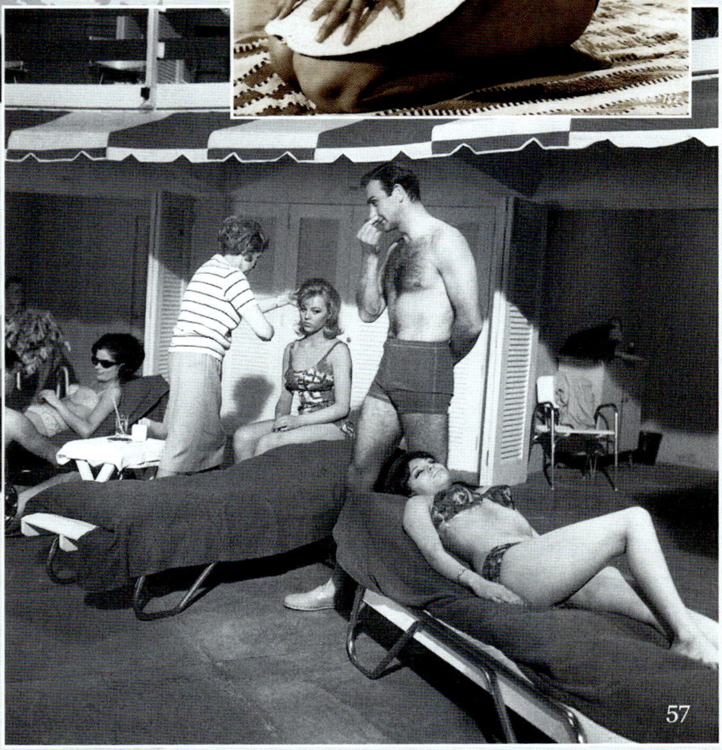

It was inevitable that George would soon get into movie work, but perhaps not so obvious that he would take his talents to the burgeoning 8mm market. 'Somebody suggested it to me and I thought it was a good idea, which of course it was. The market was vast because all the photographic shops stocked these things - Dixons were my main customer. They were ever so simple, funny little things, really - just a girl doing a striptease and that was about it.

'Of course you couldn't show anything; you had to shoot very carefully, because all you could show were tits and bums and that was about it. There was nothing written down as far as censorship was concerned. Nobody said you can do this but you can't do that. But we

Marie Devereux / RIGHT: in *The Stranglers of Bombay* (1959)

instinctively knew how far we could go without getting knocked.

'We started off making 50ft shorts, then I decided to do 75ft, 100ft and 200ft, which were 20 minutes long. Originally they were all in black and white, and then we went BIG and went into colour, which was a big thing in those days. The plots were stupid but we sold thousands a week. One of Dixon's shops next door to

Pamela Green

the Prince of Wales Theatre in Coventry Street probably sold about a thousand various titles a week. That was just one shop, remember, and we had them all over the country.'

Among the heavenly bodies that stepped in front of George's 8mm camera lens was busty June Palmer, who more often appeared in similar films for her 30-years-older hubby Arthur Powell. Also known as June Power, the 38-23-37 beauty played a stripping secret agent in *Danger Girl*, disposing of a Russian spy by chucking him onto a circular saw! In *Model Entry*, she was a stripping cat burglar breaking into George's studio to give him a free show. Though June never made it on the big screen, she can be spotted as a red-headed prostitute in Hammer's 1970 *Taste the Blood of Dracula*.

Buxom Blonde Maggie Nolan was another Marks favourite. Under the name of Vicki Kennedy, she did many shoots for Marks's *Kamera* magazine and in the 1960s, found feature fame of a sort as 'Dink', who gets a sexist pat on the bum from Sean Connery's Bond in *Goldfinger* (1963). She also managed to get Robin Askwith in a right lather (admittedly not much of an achievement) as Dawn Brakes in *Carry on Girls* and was a busty inn girl in *Witchfinder General*.

Beautiful Marie Devereux was another of Harrison's sexy stable. A regular in *Kamera* in the late 1950s, the 5'4" stunner was born in New Malden, Surrey, as Patricia Sutcliffe but seemed to suit her sizzling new French moniker better. Michael Caine introduced her to George and he was immediately smitten; she worked for him at £10 a session. Marie went on to play a prostitute in *The Womaneater* (1958), a showgirl in *Grip of the Strangler* (1958) and a village girl-cum-vampire in *The Brides of Dracula* (1962) - a role for which she had to spend three hours lying in a coffin. She later went on to play a nympho in Sam Fuller's *Shock Corridor* (1963), a movie that was banned in the UK but shown in London club cinemas with a GLC 'X' certificate.

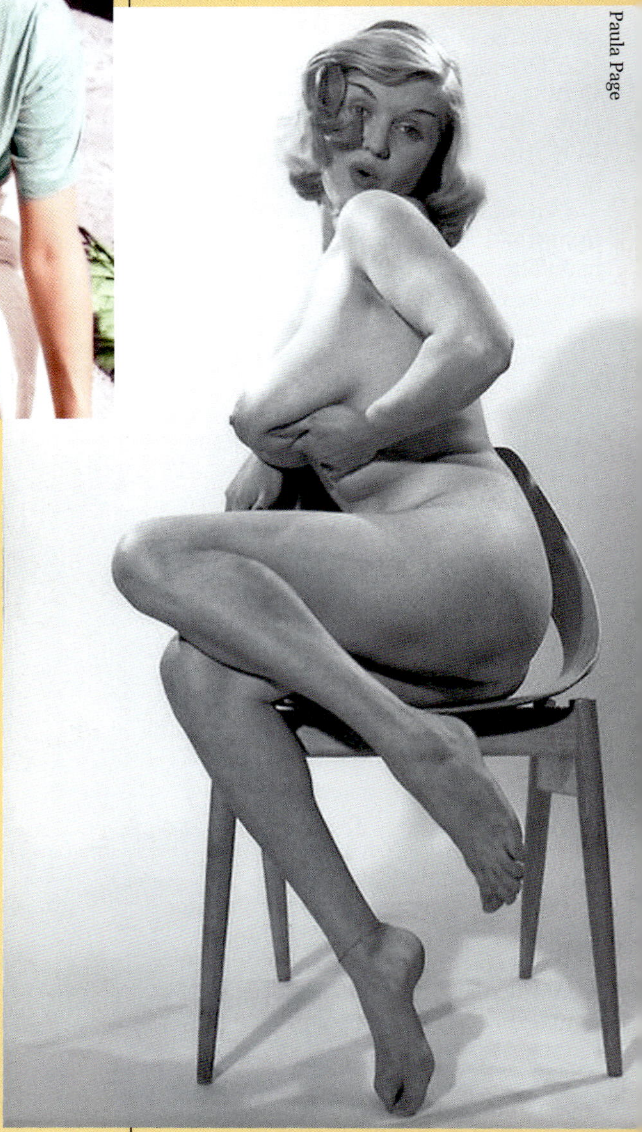

Paula Page

George told me that he loved photographing the kind of gals who could shower without getting their feet wet and the lovely Paula Page certainly thrust herself into that category. Known as 'Two Guns' Paula Page, she started her modeling career in *Fling* magazine in 1959 at the age of 18 and quickly moved on to be a *Kamera* regular. With 44E measurements, she was more stacked than a North Korean election, but her acting ability was also a bit of a bust and she never made the break into feature films.

The most famous of all of George's models, and probably the most talented too, was the lovely Pamela Green, who was born in Kingston, London, the daughter of a former merchant seaman and an amateur artist. Pamela herself seemed set for a very respectable career as an artist/designer but while studying at St Martin's School of Art, she developed a taste for nude modelling to supplement her income.

Harrison Marks and Pamela Green in *The Chimney Sweeps* (1963)

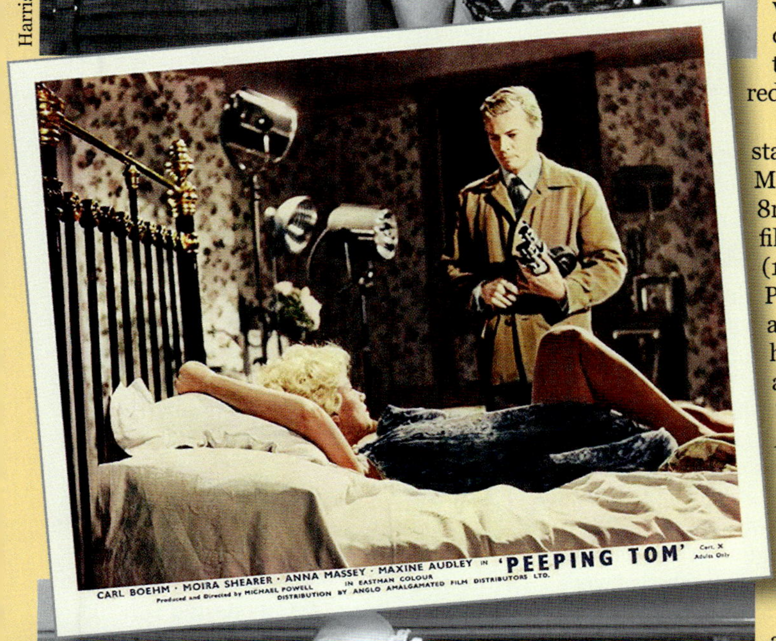

Harrison Marks and Pamela Green on the set of *The Window Dresser* (1961)

Pamela met struggling journalist/photographer Marks in 1953 when she was appearing in Paris To Piccadilly, a version of the Folies Bergère, and went into partnership with him both professionally and personally, posing for his pictures under various names and disguises, including the infamous redhead Rita Landre.

Pamela also starred in two of Marks's most popular 8mm glamour films. *Witches Brew* (1960) featured Pam as a sexy witch and George as her hunchbacked assistant, while *The Window Dresser* (1961) saw her playing a cat burglar who hides from the law (and outrageously gay shop manager Marks) by posing as a lingerie shop dummy. Her shop window striptease remains a classic, though legend has it that Marks was dragged into court on an obscenity charge because of this. The judge sensibly threw it out, saying, 'I'll buy a copy for my son, case dismissed!'

Before then, Pamela had already attracted the attention of filmmaker Michael Powell, who cast her as a model/prostitute in his landmark *Peeping Tom* (1960), Pamela's only significant mainstream credit.

Though vilified at the time of its release, *Peeping Tom* is now accepted as a disturbing, fascinating masterpiece and it certainly owes a debt of gratitude to the work of George Harrison Marks. Carl Boehm stars as Mark Lewis, a focus-puller at a film studio who is obsessed with capturing genuine fear on film. To this end, he makes 'snuff' movies, murdering prostitutes and models and making them witness their own death throes in the reflective tripod of his camera. At the same time, he carries on a relatively normal relationship with the shy young woman (Anna Massey) who lives downstairs from him with her blind mother.

To supplement his income, Lewis shoots soft porn images that are sold to 'respectable' city gents in a seedy Soho newsagent. 'He won't be doing the crossword tonight!' notes the owner, as another satisfied customer heads home for an appointment with Miss Palm and her five lovely daughters!

For the scenes showing Mark at work, Powell hired Pamela Green to portray model girl Millie, a tart with a heart who eventually falls victim to Mark's tripod (ooer!). Green later recalled that Powell visited Harrison Marks's studio in the West End and came face to face with an enormous picture of her leaning against a Parisian street wall. 'Yours truly was photographically rendered in black stockings, black high heels - and nothing else,' she said. Powell immediately turned to his art director and said, 'This is the girl I want for *Peeping Tom*.'

Green also designed the cobbled Parisian street scene she was to pose against and personally painted it brick by brick. The scene in question featured a bearded photographer who looks suspiciously like Marks himself, but it isn't him - he declined Powell's offer of a cameo, so Powell substituted a lookalike!

Naturist movies were big at the box office at the tail end of the 1950s and there was a star role for Pamela in the most famous of early British 'nudies' - Harrison Marks's first feature film, *Naked As Nature Intended*. Before filming started, Marks told the British censor, 'I'm going to be waving the banner for British nudists.' He wanted to wave a lot more than that, but the censor wasn't having it.

Funded to the tune of £3,000 by Compton Cinema Club owners Tony Tenser and Michael Klinger, *Naked as Nature Intended* was billed as 'The Greatest Nudist Film Ever!' But Green explained that Marks was required to set aside his predilection for fuller figures: 'They really weren't the type of girl he liked. They had no shape because they were going to be running about a beach. They couldn't have large breasts or they would be bouncing about all over the place!'

Filmed in September 1960, it chronicled the adventures of five young girls who escaped their hum-drum lives by going on a motoring holiday to Cornwall where they discover the joys of nudism in a

Bridget Leonard, Pamela Green, Jackie Salt and Petrina Forsyth in *As Nature Intended* (1961)

big way. They also visit Stonehenge and the Minack Open Air Theatre in Porthcurno.

Of course, pubic hair was forbidden at the time, even in magazines, where models were either shaved or had their genital area airbrushed. Thus it was that towels, bags, balls, all seemed to attach themselves to the performers as they played volleyball and frolicked in the freezing cold surf trying desperately to look like they were having a good time.

Though innocent enough to nab a PG certificate these days, the movie caused a fair amount of trouser turbulence down at the BBFC in 1960. Censor John Trevelyan objected strongly to a scene where Pamela emerged from a shower in the flat she shared with Petrina Forsyth, seen reclining in her baby doll nightdress. Trevelyan thought this suggested a lesbian relationship and removed it - the scene, that is, not the nightdress.

More modelling work followed for Pamela, as well as the odd film role in the likes of *The Day the Earth Caught Fire* (1961). She spent eight years with the womanising George before leaving him to move in with stills photographer Douglas Webb. She devoted herself to posing for Webb and assisting him in his work in various films like *The Legend Of The Werewolf* (1974) - where she had a small unbilled role as a tart - and would pop up in various popular TV shows like *The Sweeney*; it's her fingerprints that you see in the show's main credits.

Webb had a stroke in 1985 and the couple subsequently retired to the Isle of Wight, where Pamela continued to model right up to Webb's death in 1997.

Although she was generally regarded as the business brains behind the partnership with Marks, and certainly was responsible for much of the set and costume design, Green never really capitalised on her popularity as a model and mainstream success eluded her. But cult fame seems to have assured Pamela of immortality as a 'British Betty Page' and she spent her later years, until her death at the age of 81 in 2010, selling her photographs and videos.

As for George, well, he went on to make eight feature films in all. *Nine Ages of Nakedness* was the most successful, a comic fantasy in which the director himself appeared in nine different roles as our guide and host on a topless tour of man's evolution. The nudes in space finale was a highlight. The rest of the cast-list was stocked with a cut-price 'Carry On' crew of music hall comics like the late Max Bacon, Cardew Robinson, Rita Webb and Julian Orchard, as well as buxom beauties such as the aforementioned package-movie queen June Palmer.

Other Harrison Marks feature films include *The Chimney Sweeps* (1963), a rare non-sex feature which he produced and scripted, and *The Naked World of Harrison Marks*, a big production filmed in London's Holborn Studios where Marks is seen at work photographing twenty beautiful girls (including Christine Williams from *Playboy*). It's a dirty job, but someone has to do it. Marks appeared as James Bond, Al Capone and Dracula, and a voice-over narration was provided by spooky Valentine Dyall. Pamela Green made a cameo appearance.

Next came *Pattern Of Evil*, which was a sexy murder mystery made specifically for America. This one was shot on a very low budget over four or five days, and George told me that some gangsters bankrolled it. 'Halfway through the filming, in walked a guy in a loud blue-checked suit. He looked to me like a music hall comic. I asked my agent, "Is he in showbiz? He looks like a comic." He said, "Yeah, he's a really funny guy. He's got a gun in his pocket and he's with the mob!"'

Pattern of Evil has never been shown in England. It's about the bisexual owner of a London cosmetics company and suspects in a murder being put on a torture rack. Busty Monique Devereaux was one of the stars, and it was released by the same company who put out Andy Warhol's *Heat*. 'It wasn't a porn movie, but it was raunchy for its time,' said Marks. 'Mind you, I suppose if you looked at it now you'd have a good laugh! They were all successful, but *Nine Ages* was probably the biggest. It ran for seventeen months.'

Bigger still was *Come Play With Me*, the feature that George shot for *Sunday Sport* publishing tycoon David Sullivan. Among the beauties on display here were Ingmar Bergman's daughter, Anna, as well

Harrison Marks

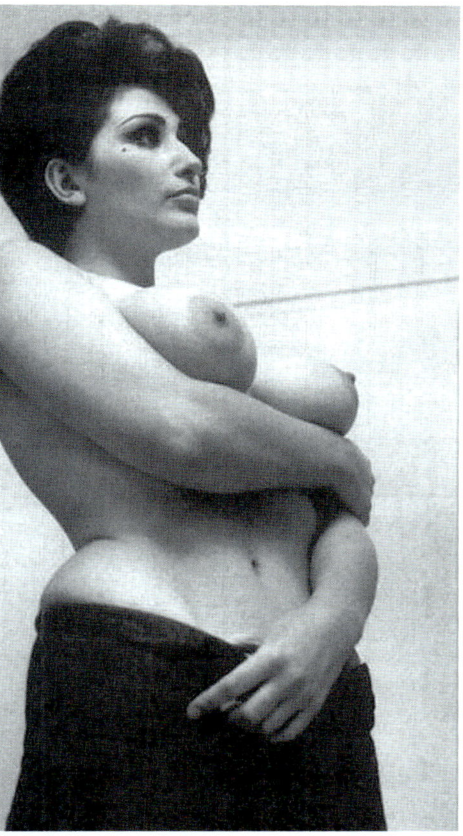
Monique Devereaux

as Benny Hill regulars Suzy Mandel and Sue Longhurst. 'That was the bonanza,' smiles George. 'It ran for three and a half years in the Moulin Cinema in Soho. David Sullivan did a very good deal with the Moulin, meaning that providing the takings for the film didn't go below a certain level, the cinema couldn't take it off. Of course, London is full of tourists so the cinema kept filling up all the time.'

The movie gave him a chance to work with top British porno icon Mary Millington, who tragically committed suicide a few years later. 'She was a sweet girl, a lovely kid,' he remembered. 'But she only had a tiny part in the film. Basically it was a comedy. I had eleven top-name comics in the thing but with tit-and-bum in it as well, which was always my trademark. In fact, that was the only one I did for Dave Sullivan. *Come Play With Me* was a very low budget production and it nearly killed me making it.' There's an apocryphal story that David Sullivan bought George's share of the profits of *Come Play With Me* for £3,000 cash when the two were out drinking together. The film went on to make millions.

After that, George decided to sit back and take it easy for a while, until a chance meeting in a Soho pub set his career off in a new direction. 'All the characters in the book game used this pub and I got quite friendly with the lads who published a very popular spanking magazine called *Janus*. One day they asked me if I would do some films for them - this was before video, incidentally. I shot four or five sets.' He chuckles loudly at this point, explaining: 'I don't understand all this spanking stuff; I thought, this has got to be a joke! I knew nothing about it at that time.

'The chap who founded the *Janus* magazine was an old fellow called Van Ocker. He was getting on a bit - in his 70s - and he was ill. The fellows that owned the magazine had no idea how to put a magazine together and didn't particularly care. As long as it made money, that was it. Anyway, one day Van Ocker snuffed it. And I was in the pub listening to these guys say, "What are we going to do? We're a month late with the magazine". Then they said, 'Hang on, George was in the publishing game for years...' They asked me to help them out, so I said take me up to the office and I'll see what I can do. I was with them for two years, during which time I realised what a marvellous and relatively untapped market it was.

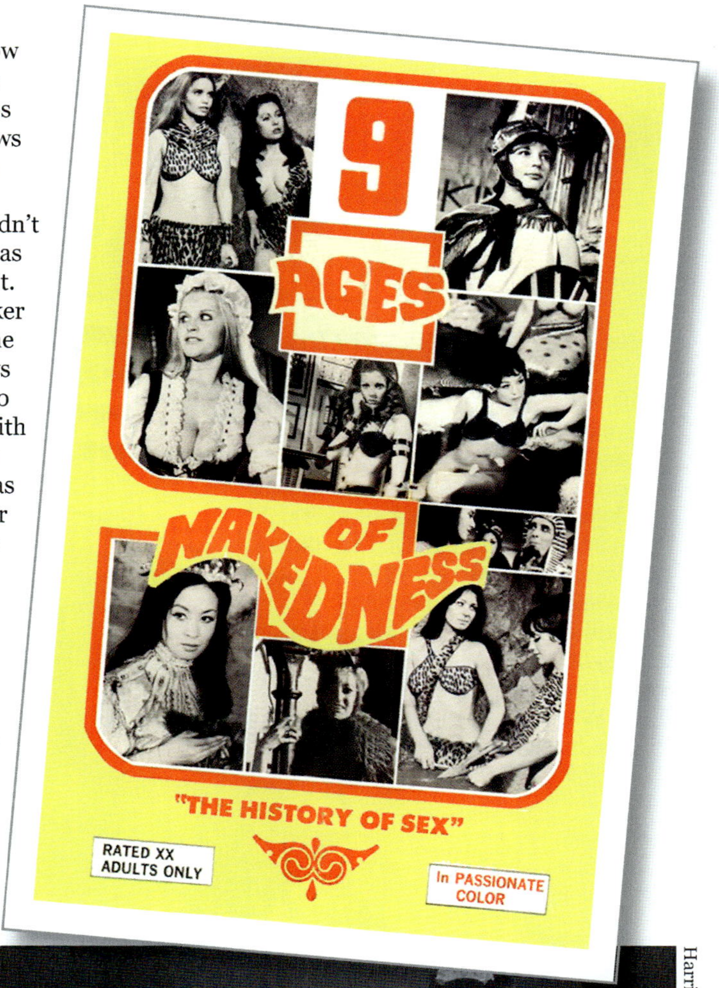

'Eventually, I decided to start my own magazine - called *Kane*. And, of course, just about that time the video market started to blossom and I started to get letters from readers asking if videos were available. I thought: I had better get into this as well!' And get into it he did. At the time I interviewed George, Kane Video had about sixty titles available and produced a new one every six to eight weeks, usually photographed 'on location' in George's opulent headquarters.

Harrison Marks on the set of *The Dream World of Harrison Marks* (1966)

'The people who buy this stuff are doctors, solicitors, barristers,' he insisted. 'It's very mild, not hardcore. Girls actually ring me up to be in them because they have so much fun. One tells another who tells another. I look at them and say, I could fit her into this, I could fit her into that. I won't use girls who are unhappy with the material. The films are not vicious. They're tongue-in-cheek and, as you can see, there's always a touch of comedy.'

Very true, in *Five of the Best*, a group of randy businessmen mete out corrective training to squealing dolly birds. A posh gent is chastising a bare-bottomed bimbo across his knee when his false moustache begins to peel away from his upper lip. Once a vaudevillian, always a vaudevillian.

George Harrison Marks died of bone cancer on June 27, 1997. He was 70 years of age and to be frank, it was amazing that he lasted so long. During his very full life, he'd been married four times and arrested and made bankrupt twice. He will be remembered as the man who brought naked women to the British High Street and his airbrushed nudes caused many a hand-reared schoolboy to grow up believing that naked women had nothing between their legs. I think you'll agree, that's quite a legacy.

KILLERS FROM SPACE

Richard Klemensen goes bug-eyed over a bevy of low-budget aliens...

'Those eyes! Those HORRIBLE eyes!'

IN life, where there are brothers, you can have one who makes a mark and succeeds; let's say Michael Corleone.. Then there is Fredo. In the film business, some brothers both have successful careers - Robert and Curtis Siodmak, for instance. Then there's Billy Wilder and... W Lee Wilder.

While younger brother Billy was writing and directing such films as *Double Indemnity*, *Sunset Boulevard* and *Some Like it Hot*, W Lee was making spiritual music shorts.

Barbara Bestar

Actually, W Lee also began, and stayed, in the area of 'B' movies - starting out in 1945 as the producer of *The Great Flamarion*, directed by Anthony Mann for Republic Pictures. But for most of his career, he wrote, produced and directed - often for his own production company, Planet Filmplays - low- budget and low expectation movies.

Such was the case in 1953. While sibling Billy was filming *Stalag 17* - which would win William Holden a Best Actor Oscar - W Lee wasshooting The *Man Who Saved the Earth* (later retitled *Killers From Space*). Interestingly enough, both films would offer starring roles to the younger brother of James Arness - Peter Graves. Filming began in July 1953 at KTTV Studios (formerly the Nassour Studios).

Killers From Space starts with an atomic bomb test at Soledad Flats (no such place exists in life). Through a mishmash of unrelated stock-footage shots - including the same bomber that is shown as both jet and prop-driven, and a fighter that changes from shot to shot - we are introduced to Dr Douglas Martin (Graves). He is a scientist who is engaged in flying over the mushroom cloud to conduct a series of tests. While staring down at the seat of the explosion, he spies something gleaming on the ground. Suddenly, he and his co-pilot become trapped when their plane starts to spiral towards the ground, where it crashes.

Another mix of different stock-footage helicopters, supposed representing just one, takes off for the site. When the rescuers arrive at crash central, they find the dead co-pilot but no Dr Martin. Later, Martin comes stumbling up to the base, appearing unhurt except for a long, cross-shaped, scar on his chest. He can't remember what happened or how the scar got there. He is nevertheless given a clean bill of health and sent home to his wife to recover. (Barbara Bestar, who plays the wife, had a film career which came and went pretty quickly.)

Anyway, Martin is determined to find out when the next atomic bomb test will be held. But the higher-ups at US Air Force command are wary of him (is he the *real* Doc Martin!? - turns out, he is) and have called in the FBI to investigate. There is another bomb test, and Martin takes the opportunity to steal the results and head out to the flats, where he is stopped in the act of hiding them under a rock by an FBI agent. A fight ensues, but Martin gets the upper hand and escapes. Not for long; he crashes his car and is hauled back to the base.

Back at said base, Martin is given a dose of 'truth serum' and we finally find out about th 'killers from space'. These aliens, hiding in underground caves, are from the planet Astron Delta - a dying planet. It is actually their sun that is dying and they had already uprooted from one planet to another to be closer to it. But now the sun is almost gone. A TV screen of sorts shows the spaceships flying back and forth, and some of the alien cities and landscape - not exactly world-beating in terms of effects but the most ingenious shots in the movie.

(The most notable feature of the 'killers from space' is their infamous bulging eyes, which look like ping-pong balls cut in two. According to makeup man Harry Thomas, he hooked strings to the 'eyes' of the alien leader to allow them to move back and forth!)

Martin is told that he was brought back from the dead (which explains the less than exemplary bit of surgery on his chest) to help the folks from Astron Delta in their quest to rid Earth of its inhabitants, using irradiated giant insects, spiders, lizards and other creepy-crawlies. (There follows a long section of pretty dicey rear projection as Martin runs back and forth through the cave area while being chased by the critters, until he is rescued by alien leader Denab.)

Despite that fact that Martin has spilled the beans to the authorities via a 'truth serum', no one at the base believes a word that he's said. So left to his own devices, he figures out that cutting off all the electrical power to the area for ten seconds will short-circuit the Astron Deltans' plans. He breaks out and heads towards the local power plant (according to Graves, in conversation with Tom Weaver, 'The power plant was the LA Department of Water and Power, their big power generating plant down in Long Beach, where they use seawater and the tides to run their machinery.') After being chased all over the plant, he manages to hold the FBI at gunpoint and cut the power for the requisite ten seconds. The ground shakes and explosions are heard. Our heroic group watch through a window as another mushroom cloud rises in the air... Scratch the Astron Deltans.

W Lee Wilder had made all of his recent films for United Artists (on a financing setup) but according to his son, Myles, who wrote the script, *Killers From Space* was funded using his father's own money. And there were no sets built: all the offices on show were those of W Lee at KTTV - which is pretty apparent, as everything is minimally dressed, bland and boring to look at.

The film was originally intended, by RKO, to go out under the title of *Target Earth*. However, producer Herman Cohen was planning to use that same title for his upcoming Richard Denning sci-fi opus.

Cohen convinced RKO to change to *Killers From Space*.

The leading man was, as mentioned, Peter Graves - a tall, fairly talented actor, whose career spanned from 1951 to 2010, the year of his death. He is best known for his six years top-lining the original *Mission: Impossible* series on television, along with a latterday career resurgence in the *Airplane* comedies. He never stopped working. Nor did he ever complain, or put down, being identified with the low budget sci-fi schlock of the 1950s. 'This is work. This will get my face on the screen. This will give me more experience as an actor,' he remarked. 'Even if I hadn't had a family at the time, I would have done it. I wasn't doing anything else.'

'If I had been really convinced at the time that doing three or four science-fiction pictures on the cheapie side would not develop my career, perhaps I might not have done 'em. Maybe I'd have gone to New York and done a play or something. But.. that's the path I took and so be it.'

Graves also had some

interesting comments to make in interview with Tom Weaver: 'KTTV was just down the hill from Bronson Caverns. Bronson Caverns was one of the most famous movie locations in the business. There was such a variety of stuff there, and it was right down the hill from Hollywood Boulevard a couple of miles. The caves had been made by guys who were mining or drilling for something. A clever man with a camera could make it look like the dwelling places of aliens or a subterranean world beneath Africa...'

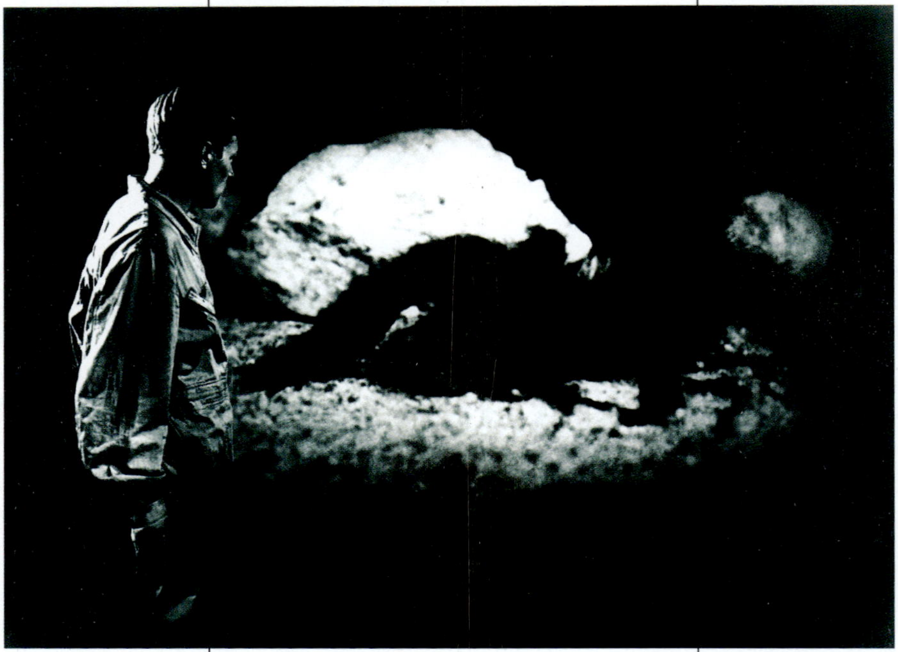

But the bug-eyed aliens are the thing most viewers remember from *Killers From Space* - their eyes having 'evolved' to deal with the decreasing light as their sun died. Makeup man Harry Thomas recalled how they came to be: 'The producer-director W Lee Wilder wanted to get ping-pong balls and cut them for the eyes of the aliens, because he didn't want to pay the price I asked, which wasn't very much. I made the eyes out of plastic and coloured them, gave them a light film for the sclera and cut a hole in the middle so the actor could see. What I wanted to do was punch the plastic eyes through cotton or lens paper, then seal all that to the face so it would look like they came out of the eye sockets themselves. They wouldn't give me that time, nor time to shade the sides of the eyes to give some dimension and feelings'.

The overall look of the aliens is not too bad, although most of the action involves them simply walking or running aimlessly down the same tunnels. In the same way, much of the action on the surface involves cars merely driving here and there. The amount of stock footage used is high, even for a low-budget movie of the time; according to Myles Wilder, the whole thing only took six days to shoot. Aside from Graves, the actors were a group who worked mainly on low-budget movies and TV. Frank Gerstel, who played Dr Kruger, ran up a total of 199 acting credits during his career - and Gerstel only lived to 54!

Killers from Space is not entirely awful. It was professionally produced and released - although the IMDb lists an alarming number of goofs and continuity errors. But the film has nothing much to recommend it other than the curious sight of guys in Republic-style alien costumes with ping-pong balls glued over their eyes. RKO Radio released it in 1954, as did General Film Distributors in the UK the same year.

According to Graves, who worked with both W Lee and Billy Wilder (Grave played a key role in 1950's *Stalag 17*), the brothers did not particularly get along or even talk much. Perhaps if they had, some of the the talent that Billy Wilder continually showed throughout his long and illustrious career might have been passed onto his sibling.

Then again, perhaps not...

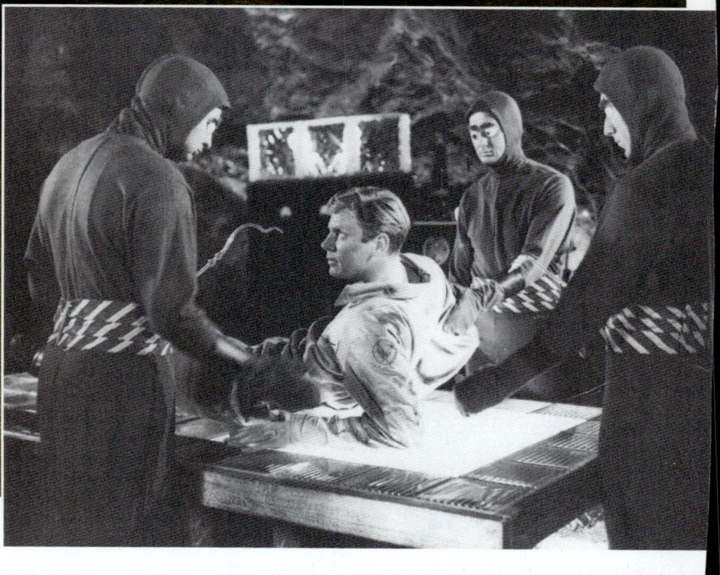